Flawed Families
of the Bible

Flawed Families
of the Bible

How God's Grace Works
through Imperfect Relationships

David E. Garland
and Diana R. Garland

BrazosPress
Grand Rapids, Michigan

© 2007 by David E. Garland and Diana R. Garland

Published by Brazos Press
a division of Baker Publishing Group
P.O. Box 6287, Grand Rapids, MI 49516-6287
www.brazospress.com

Printed in the United States of America

Library of Congress Cataloging-in-Publication Data
Garland, David E.
    Flawed families of the Bible : how God's grace works through imperfect relationships / David E. Garland and Diana R. Garland.
        p.   cm.
    Includes bibliographical references.
    ISBN 10: 1-58743-155-6 (pbk.)
    ISBN 978-1-58743-155-5 (pbk.)
    1. Family—Biblical teaching. 2. Bible O.T.—Biography. I. Garland, Diana S. Richmond, 1950– II. Title.
BS1199.F32G37 2007
220.9′2—dc22   2006027979

For Dorsie Richmond, in gratitude for a lifetime of unwavering love and support.

Acknowledgment

We are grateful to the Lilly Endowment, Inc., for generous financial support of the Congregational Resources Project. This book is one of several in the Families and Faith series published by that project.

Contents

Introduction

Most Christians believe that they can go to the Bible for guidance for living their daily family lives. A large portion of the Bible, particularly the Old Testament, consists of stories about families. In Numbers 21:14 there is a reference to "the Book of the Wars of the LORD," but this book about battles apparently has been lost. What have been preserved are the stories about families. It is as if to say that stories of God working in battles are less important than the stories of God working in families. Even the battle stories that have been preserved, such as that of David and Goliath, are told in the context of the human relationships of families—in this case, the family of Saul and David and his brothers.

Many of the Bible's family stories, however, do not always seem edifying and often do not seem suitable for emulating. Many of the stories in scripture behind the genealogies of Jesus recorded in Matthew 1:1–17 and Luke 3:23–38 are steamy and violent, even by today's standards. The family tree of the Messiah reveals a family whose closets seem to be bursting with skeletons. Since their stories are told in the Bible, their closets are wide open for everyone to peer into. If this family history leads to the coming of Christ as the fulfillment of God's promises, then one might say that God writes with very crooked lines. In these and other stories of the lives of families, we discover weak, scarred, scared, struggling, failing people who have suffered and survived horrible ordeals, many of them self-inflicted. Yet God used them.

For some of us, the Sunday school lessons printed in the "quarterlies" of our childhood began with the one-sentence "central truth" of the lesson, which was always printed just below the title and Bible passages for that day. But the actual biblical narratives do not begin or end with a "central truth." Instead, they invite us to wonder and explore, even to struggle with the story before us and seek its meaning as it intersects with our own life story. The Book of Proverbs captures many of the truths that can be learned from these stories and expresses them in pithy warnings:

> Under three things the earth trembles; under four it cannot bear up: . . . an unloved woman when she gets a husband, and a maid when she succeeds her mistress. (Prov. 30:21, 23)

> Foolish children are a grief to their father and bitterness to her who bore them. (Prov. 17:25)

> So is he who sleeps with his neighbor's wife; no one who touches her will go unpunished. (Prov. 6:29)

> Discipline your children, and they will give you rest; they will give delight to your heart. (Prov. 29:17)

The stories of Abraham, Sarah, and Hagar, David and Bathsheba, Jacob and his sons, and David and his sons Amnon and Absalom illustrate these truths, and they communicate things that cannot be communicated by proverbs. Their stories hold much more power than the preceding proverbs do, because they invite us into the complexities and depths of life as we experience it. We can see our own conflicts and problems and may even find comfort in seeing ourselves in the company of these ancient family members of Jesus. If we think our lives are a mess, look at what they went through! And God never abandoned them. God's grace somehow managed to work through all of their imperfections. Perhaps we can lean, then, on the promise that God's grace will never leave *us*, and even trust that God is working through our struggles.

The stories in the Bible pack a punch, but many Christians do not know them. Some Christians were not raised with Sunday school memory verses and didn't have those quarterlies to study each week. If they pick up the Bible to read it and delve past how many cubits measure what and the lists of names with all the begats, they discover that much of it is perplexing and hard to understand. Why did God ask Abraham to sacrifice his son Isaac? Why would God cherish an adulterer and murderer like David? Why did God not intervene more directly and more often to set these people straight? As the Ethiopian eunuch said, "How can I [understand], unless someone guides me?" (Acts 8:31). How do these stories about family woes tie into our contemporary world?

The stories of families in the Bible are raw and uncensored, bitter reminders of how awful family life can become. Though the ancient families of the Bible lived in a distant time, in a far-off place, with social customs and rules that sometimes mystify us, when we peel back the surface differences, we discover that people and their family problems seem not to have changed much at all. Once we begin to understand them, their stories and experiences may seem to mirror our own lives. We can see reflections of ourselves in their messy and troubled escapades.

These stories are vital to our understanding of God, our faith, ourselves, and our world. Bible stories portray real flesh-and-blood human beings struggling with their past history and with their fallibilities and sinfulness. They battle for their present survival and a future for themselves and for their children and their children's children. The twists and turns of relationships and the brokenness of being fallen humans are all there in these stories. Yet it is in those broken places that we catch glimpses of God's grace and healing, of God silently reaching in to touch the wound, and often, of fragile and broken people stepping up to do what is right.

That is the overarching theme of this book—a theme of hope and grace for families. Richard Rohr tells a story of Navajo rug weaving (1995, 18). These beautifully handcrafted rugs are perfectly structured, except for a corner on each rug where an obvious flaw can be found. An inquiry about why all the rugs have an out-of-place thread was met with the reply, "This is where the spirit moves in and out." Our families and the families in ancient Israel are flawed by dismemberment, physical and emotional violence, infidelity, petty jealousies, and mean-spiritedness. They are far from perfect. Yet it is exactly in those flawed places that the Spirit of God moves and where we can catch a glimpse of grace.

A lovely sculpture by Sheila Oettinger is found in a park in Normal, Illinois: a husband and wife embrace and look lovingly into each other's eyes while their toddler son lies between them in his mother's lap, looking up trustingly at his parents, as his older sister, lying on her mother's leg, looks dreamingly into the distance. It is entitled, "The Normal Family." It is the "norm" only in our imaginations. It certainly does not capture the biblical families that we will discuss. Rather, it illustrates the idol that we cling to, and the contrast between the imagined ideal and our own real life experiences can cause us grief. As one woman has said, "The only thing normal in our family is the knob that says Normal on the clothes dryer." The sculpture has suffered from repeated vandalism, perhaps by those striking out at an image that seems to judge negatively any whose families might look different. The French novelist, André Gide, in *Les Nouvelles nourritures,* bitterly expressed a forlorn attitude shared by many: "Families! I hate you! Shut-in homes, closed doors, jealous possessors of happiness."

We do not attempt to distill from the accounts of biblical families three easy steps to leading a happy family life, or six ways to avoid the pitfalls leading to family disaster. Instead, we dig into the complexities and difficulties of their lives to try to understand them and, through them, God's ways of working in their broken places. We have taught these stories in church settings and have discovered that it is best to let them, as scripture, do their work through the power of the Holy Spirit. We seek to hear the sometimes silenced voices of members of God's family who have been ignored over the centuries.

Each chapter in this book will explore the stories of one of the families in the Bible, seeking to make connections to the experiences of families today. We will tell their stories in such a way as to encourage families to tell their own stories of faith—to one another, and to the congregational community. It is in telling our stories to one another—stories of defeats as well as of victories, of fallenness as well as of graces—that we can truly know one another, walk with one another, and be community for one another. These ancient families have shared their stories with other people walking the same path of faith for thousands of years, and through that sharing, families walking behind them have glimpsed the sacred woven into their everyday struggles and life crises. Through the connections between the stories of the ancients and our own stories, God's sacred story continues to unfold. Similarly, even and especially as we share with one another in a community of faith our stories of brokenness and healing, of sinfulness and grace, we too can call out the sacred thread in one another's lives. It is not the case that anything goes when it comes to family, but the evidence is that God has always used broken, messed-up families—almost in spite of themselves.

What purpose does it serve for God to have used such flawed and broken families? Surely there were some families that looked at least somewhat more like Oettinger's sculpture. The apostle Paul later explained that God's treasure is carried in clay pots (2 Cor. 4:7). Clay pots are not only cheap and plain, but they are often flawed and easily broken. Paul was referring to himself, and he often pointed to his own weakness and sinfulness.

What is the point of putting treasure in a cheap pot? What happens when beautiful flowers are put in a plain and cracked coffee cup? All the attention then goes to the flowers themselves. One's focus is not diverted from what is supposed to be the message of beauty by the carrying case. But it is even more than that. When we are strong and courageous and do something that is admirable, then we take credit for it. "Look, Mom, what I did!" is a message we carry in our hearts even as grown-up children. We want to feel strong and wise and courageous. But when we do something we know is beyond our own abilities or face a challenge with strength and courage that we know we didn't have on our own, then we wonder how we had such strength. Where does such strength come from? It doesn't come from the mountains of self-help books or some reserve of inner fortitude. It comes from God. When God chooses the plain, the ordinary, the weak, and the broken, God's power stands out more clearly.

God likes to work through prophets like Moses, who had a speech impediment and a problem with his temper. God worked through a young Hebrew maiden, Esther, to stave off the annihilation of the Jewish people by the Persian king. God used a little boy with some rocks and a slingshot to fell a ten-foot giant. God used a little boy's fish sandwich to feed thousands of people. God used a few women as the first voices to proclaim the resurrection of the Son of God. None of these little people were successful on their own. They were not strong enough or wise enough or resourceful enough to be responsible for what they did. God was responsible. God used them. They simply relied on God's grace and were faithful to act in ways they were called to act despite their life circumstances. And that was enough.

In 2 Corinthians 4:8–9, Paul describes himself as "hard pressed on every side, but not crushed; perplexed, but not in despair; persecuted but not abandoned; struck down, but not destroyed" (TNIV). He was under great pressure, "far beyond our ability to endure" (1:8). Clay pots are brittle, easily cracked, sometimes shattered. Paul's afflictions caused some stress fractures. The knocks and bangs during his ministry caused some cracks in the earthen vessel. Paul, the earthen vessel, remained intact not because of his own strength and capability but because of the sustaining power of God. He was held together by divine glue.

In fact, it is not flowers but a brilliant treasure of jewels—the truth of God—that is carried in clay pots. Those shimmering jewels actually shine through the cracks. It is in the brokenness that the truth about God's grace shines through. God's family is a whole series of cracked pots, not beautiful sculptures. Their stories are not simple but instead reveal how God works through darkness and struggle, through shattered lives. God's grace often seems hidden, like yeast that silently and imperceptibly brings about change in and through us. We find hope for ourselves not in the beautiful, bigger-than-life statue of a perfect family but rather in the twists and turns and plunges into crises in these stories of very "normal" biblical family relationships.

1

Sarah's and Hagar's Stories
Hope versus Hopelessness

Desperate to Be a Person of Worth (Genesis 12:1–9)

Sarai was barren for so many years that she had forgotten when it was that she had given up all hope of bearing children. She hoped long ago when her husband, Abram, told her that God had promised to make a great nation from Abram's children (Gen. 12:2). The years flew by, then they slowed to a crawl, and nothing happened. Abram was now seventy-five (Gen. 12:4), and Sarai was ten years younger (Gen. 17:17), long past the time in life for having children. Sarai was expected to have second-hand faith—faith in God's promise to Abram, and also faith that her husband really heard God speaking to him this promise. Her biological clock had run down long ago, and she probably wondered if her husband had simply fallen asleep and dreamed up this conversation with God.

Once again, years after the first promise, God had come to Abram in a vision and assured him, "Do not be afraid, Abram! I am your shield and will give you a very great reward!" Abram was a bit huffy at this latest word from God. "What good are your gifts, since I am still childless, in case you haven't noticed! Sarai and I have given up on your promises, and I have made my servant Eliezer of Damascus my heir" (Gen. 15:1–3, authors' paraphrase). God said that was not the plan, but that he would have an heir who was his own issue. Abram's discouragement turned into belief once again, and because he put his faith in God, "the Lord reckoned it to him as righteousness" (Gen. 15:6). It was a pronouncement that Paul would seize upon centuries later (Gal. 3:6; Rom. 4:3). Faith is anchored in divine promise, not human possibility.

God told Abram to look up in the sky and count the stars, if he could, and said his descendants would be just about that many. God then told him about their future and talked more about the Promised Land. And Abram believed, and told Sarai about this renewed promised from God.

Yet the years kept on passing, and no baby announcements needed to be ordered. Perhaps Sarai was frustrated that God did not include her in the pronouncement. She had to rely on Abram's word. Perhaps she wondered if old Abram was just using his so-called word from God as an entrée to her bed: "Come on, Sarai, God made a promise, so we need to provide the way."

The opening verse of Genesis 16 rubs it in: "Now Sarai, Abram's wife, bore him no children." She had failed in her woman's role of marrying and bearing children—male children. English synonyms for the word *barren* such as *unproduc-*

tive, unsuccessful, fruitless, desolate, and *dry* convey how Sarai would have been regarded and would have felt in her context. No woman back then would have *chosen* not to have children, so in the minds of everyone around her, she was a failure as a woman. Did other women tease her about her failure? Or whisper behind her back? She suffered, the way women who are unwillingly childless today suffer when others thoughtlessly ask them, "When are you having kids?" or exclaim with an air of condescension, "Just wait till *you* have kids! You'll understand better then what it's like." We can imagine this conversation earlier when Sarai and Abram pulled up stakes from Ur of the Chaldees after deciding to obey God's call and move on (Gen. 12:1–5). A neighbor might have asked, "Sarai, why are you moving?"

"Well, Abe thinks that this is not the best place to raise the kids."

"What kids? You don't have any kids! And surely it's too late for you to start now!"

She had moved with her husband, obeying God's call, and listened to tales about his conversations with God, but Sarai's life was still "barren."

As painful as the judgment of others might have felt for Sarai, it was her own keen disappointment that hurt the most. She probably longed not only for the fulfillment of being a mother but also for the honor and respect accorded to mothers in a society where women did not count for much otherwise. We know now that male infertility can be the cause for the failure to conceive, but there was no such biological knowledge in Sarai's world. Sarai's identity as a woman, as someone of worth, depended on her producing and nursing babies. She did not gain value in men's eyes by being a righteous and faithful human being but by producing male heirs for her husband. An empty womb meant an empty life.

Women modeled themselves on the dreams and expectations of men, as many still do today. Validation of her worth came from without, from the approval of her husband.

Until she bore children, she could not help but feel that she was incomplete and, worse, that she was being judged by God for some unknown sin. She was the woman standing in Abram's shadow. He had the privilege of talking with God and hearing all these great promises. He dutifully shared the news with her, and yet nothing came to pass. She remained childless. She must have wondered whether her husband did not begin to think that she was a liability, that she was the reason that the promise was not yet fulfilled. Did he wish he had traded her in long ago? What she may not have realized was that while the promise was to Abram, it was a promise to her as well. God had just as surely chosen Sarai as he had chosen Abram.

God Protects Sarai (Genesis 15:10–20)

One incident should have driven home to Sarai that she also was chosen by God. She probably would have liked to forget the time when Abram took the family to Egypt to escape famine in the land and told her, "Look, you are one beautiful woman. When the Egyptians get a look at you, they are going to want to kill me to get you. Please tell them you are my sister. Then they will treat me well and will spare my life just to keep you happy" (Gen. 12:10–13, authors' paraphrase). Abram seemed to care only about being treated well himself—not about what might happen to Sarai. Abram used her as a shield, putting her at great risk to protect himself. Knowing that she was beautiful and would be the object of attraction to other men, Abram had her masquerade as an available single woman.

Abram's plan was successful. As he had suspected, Sarai indeed caught the eye of Pharaoh's spies, and Pharaoh followed up by inviting her into his household and adding her to his collection of concubines. He showed his appreciation to Abram by showering him with "sheep, oxen, male donkeys, male and female slaves, female donkeys and camels" (Gen. 12:16). Like an ancient sex trader, Abram became wealthy essentially by selling Sarai to another man. What it was like for Sarai to be a concubine in Pharaoh's house, the text does not say. One can guess, however, and she probably did not have warm thoughts toward her husband for putting her in this predicament as the newest member of the king's harem.

Why did Sarai agree to this crazy plan? Evidently, she had believed Abram when he said he was in danger, and she wanted to protect him from possible harm. Or their relationship was such that she could not argue with him. If she did not want to cooperate, then surely she could have mentioned to someone that she was Abram's wife, not his sister. Instead, she honored his wishes and was willing to sacrifice herself in this way for him.

The Lord was not consulted about this plan and did not like it, to say the least. As an expression of divine displeasure, the Lord inflicted on Pharaoh and his household a plague of terrible diseases. God acted in behalf of Sarai, because God is the God who acts with justice and compassion for those who are mistreated and struggling.

If she had reflected on it, Sarai should have realized as the plague descended on Egypt that she also had been chosen by God to fulfill the promise given to Abram. God had protected her in this awful situation, while Abram, her husband, had not. If the situation had been left up to Abram, the promise would have been lost, handed over with Sarai to an Egyptian potentate. Abram had no plan for rescuing Sarai from the Pharaoh's harem; evidently, he would have just left her there. The promise of a multitude of descendants would have had to take place through another woman. God had evidently planned on Sarai, however, so the situation was not left solely to Abram and some lustful ruler of Egypt. God intervened to rescue both Sarai and the promise that Abram selfishly put at such risk.

Somehow, Pharaoh discerned that the plagues were caused by his newest addition to the women's quarters. How he found out the truth we do not know; did Sarai tell? Find out he did, and he confronted Abram about the ruse. "What is this you have done to me? She is not your sister, you liar! She is your wife? Why did you do this to me? Here she is—your wife. Take her and get out of here!" So Pharaoh sent Abram away with his wife and all his possessions (Gen. 12:18–20, authors' paraphrase), hoping that would remedy the pestilence. Probably the only reason that Pharaoh did not kill Abram on the spot was his fear that something even worse than the decimating plague of diseases might fall on their heads.

Abram walked away with his wife and all the livestock and slaves Pharaoh showered upon him, probably thinking to himself, "This worked pretty well. I should try it again sometime," which, in fact, he did (see Gen. 20:1–20). How it worked for Sarai, we aren't told. Surely, it shook her trust. She must have realized how precarious her place was with a husband who would come up with a scheme like this one. It probably did not do much to fan the flames of her ardor for Abram either. But they were certainly materially richer as a result. And among their added riches was the slave-girl Hagar, who became Sarai's personal maidservant.

Trying to Find a Way through the Fog (Genesis 16:1–4)

Abram and Sarai probably did not fully realize at the time how God saved them and saved the line that would follow from them as God had promised. We often see God working only by looking back at the events of our lives. The promise was saved, but it was still just a promise. Why was it taking God so long to launch this new nation? And why had God allowed a famine, which drove them from Canaan to Egypt in the first place and put Sarai in this peril—and risked the promise? The promise was not yet realized. It was a story that had to be unfolded and lived, walking step by step in faith where they could not see. Anna Quindlen has said, "Life is not so much about beginnings and endings as it is about going on and on and on. It is about muddling through the middle." Abram and Sarai would muddle on through life, trying to find their way, waiting for God's promise to be fulfilled, and sometimes feeling worn out by it all.

Waiting is not something most people do well, neither is it something experienced with great joy and gladness. Instead, we tell ourselves and one another to do something. "Don't just sit there like a bump on a log. Take control!" Henri Nouwen says that most of us have such a hard time waiting for things to happen because of our desire "to do the things that will make the desired events take place to satisfy our wishes." He says, "For this reason, a lot of our waiting is not open-ended. Instead, our waiting is a way of controlling the future" (Nouwen 2001, 100). We see this tendency in Abraham and Sarai. They tried to control their future rather than wait on God. They could not quite bring themselves to discard their fears and their wishes for things to turn out just the way they wanted them and live in open-ended hope that allowed God to define their future.

The promise would be fulfilled, however. The descendants of Abram and Sarai would again go down to Egypt to escape famine. As God told Abram in a dream, they would be there as strangers and slaves for four hundred years, and then they would come out again with great possessions to make the journey to Canaan (Gen. 15:12–15). And Moses would lead them in this promise.

A fast-forward to the life of Moses gives us some insight into the long, long wait that characterized Abram and Sarai's life. When Moses faced the task before him, he experienced the same incredulity that Sarai had and doubted that the promise would ever come to pass. The people had been wandering in the desert, and God was telling Moses to head on into the Promised Land (Exodus 33). Moses said to the Lord,

> You have been telling me, "Lead these people," but you have not let me know whom you will send with me. You have said, "I know you by name and you have found favor with me." If you are pleased with me, teach me your ways so I may know you and continue to find favor with you. Remember that this nation is *your* people. (Exod. 33: 12–13, NIV, emphasis added)

Moses too was uncertain about the future. He and the people with him had come this far, but where was he going to find others to be his partners in this huge task of finding a home for the people? "After all," he said, "these aren't my people, these are your people, God. This is your journey, God, so show me how to tackle this future." Moses asked to see God because he wanted to know how to live into the future.

Moses had agreed to follow God so far, and God had guided him—with a cloud that went before them. When God guides people, God does not hand them a clearly marked road map instructing them to turn here, to take this exit, to follow this street. God says, "Follow this cloud." What is it like to follow a cloud? A cloud on the ground is *fog*. They could not see ahead of them. Following God in this earthly life requires walking behind and sometimes feels like plodding through a fog. We can see just far enough to know where to put our feet next, but we have no idea where we are going. We go by faith, not by sight.

Several years ago when we lived in Kentucky, we were driving to a town in Ohio near Cincinnati one early spring morning. We drove north through the Kentucky hills and then turned to go down into the Ohio River valley and across the river. And as we went down, we hit fog—dense, impenetrable fog. We inched along just barely able to make out the yellow line of the side of the road just in front of us. And there it was, just by the right front bumper—the first pillar that we knew was a part of the bridge over that huge river. We could just see the beginning posts of that bridge, and a nothingness that we knew from memory dropped to water hundreds of feet below. The bridge began on a hillside far above the water and went to—the other side? Who could see? We just had to trust that bridge still went all the way to the other side. C. S. Lewis wrote in a private letter, "A glimpse is not a vision. But to a man on a mountain road by night, a glimpse of the next three feet of road is more important and useful than a view of the horizon" (Vanauken 1977, 101–2). We had been on that road before, but Moses was standing on the end of a bridge he had never been on before, and where it ended he knew not. God showed him only the next three feet.

In fact, the answer to Moses's outcry for a clearer vision was even stranger. "Let me see you, God!" Moses cried out. "Show me where in this world you are leading me!" God said to Moses, "Okay, I'll let you see." So God placed Moses in the cleft of a rock and covered him over until God had passed by.

Only then could Moses see—not God's face, not God right there with him, but just God's backside (Exod. 33:18–23). An ancient rabbi commenting on this text says that it means that we can discover God in our lives only as we look where God has been, but we cannot see where God will be in the future, or even where God is right now.

We cannot see into a future with God as some claim to do with their horoscopes and Tarot cards. We can see only the past. Only in looking back do we begin to recognize God's presence in and through the working of our days and God's utter faithfulness. The further we go back in our memory, the more we see patterns full of meaning and purpose—but not right now, and certainly not tomorrow or the next day. We can only see where God has already been in our lives and step in faith toward the fog of the future. We can look back and understand, but never forward to know with certainty where God is leading us.

Like Moses, Sarai looked forward, and she could see nothing. She was old and getting more feeble each day. God kept encouraging them to believe the promise, but who could fault her for taking God's promise with a grain of salt or to think that she had blown it somehow? In her culture, and Sarai had no reason to doubt it, a sonless woman was believed to have in some way incurred divine displeasure. Childlessness was punishment. God was angry with Sarai for some reason. What that reason might have been was anyone's guess, but the proof was evident for all to see. She had no child, and she was an old woman. She lamented to Abram, "God has done this to me. The Lord has shut up my womb" (Gen. 16:2, authors' paraphrase).

Sarai had faithfully protected Abram and survived his abandoning her to Pharaoh's harem. But this experience must have damaged immeasurably her belief in her own worth.

Her husband cared so little for her that he would give her up to protect himself from some perceived threat. If Abram had tried to reassure her before that he loved her despite her childlessness, that reassurance seemed empty now. Sarai seemed enveloped in a heavy cloud that hid the way forward, so she made up her own path.

What options were there? Surely Abram was wondering, too. Perhaps, he thought, the promise of heirs for Abram had not meant that Sarai would be the mother. Abram could divorce her and marry another. Or he could take on additional wives if he could manage the finances. To fend off these options and to find a way to force the promise's fulfillment, Sarai came up with her own scheme. She proposed to Abram that they go the surrogate-motherhood route. Her Egyptian slave-girl, Hagar, could be her stand-in. She instructed Abram, "Go in to my slave-girl; it may be that I shall obtain children by her" (Gen. 16:2). Abram listened to the voice of Sarai rather than to the voice of God (Gen. 16:2), perhaps because hers was louder and more shrill as she campaigned to get a child. It would become one more example of the futility of humans trying to attain God's blessing and achieve God's purposes by their own machinations.

Abram had not been passive in the marriage up to this point. He had led, and she had followed. He had told her what God wanted them to do, and she had done what he said. He agreed with Sarai now because he wanted to. Whether he agreed with Sarai that this might be a way to move God's plan along or he simply was willing to be sexually involved with this younger slave—or both—we do not know. Maybe he convinced himself that this was what God had in mind all along, and he and Sarai had been slow in thinking of it. He went in to Hagar, and she conceived. Abram would be eighty-six years old when he first became a father.

Hagar's child would become Sarai's, and then everything would be fine for Sarai. Hagar was just a slave and had no rights. As a slave, she was regarded as both the property and the legal extension of her mistress. She did not get a vote in this decision. Once again, a woman had no say in the plan and became a pawn in the selfish schemes of others. We have no idea how Hagar felt about this plan. She was the handmaiden of her mistress. They spent a great deal of time together, but what was their relationship like? Did Sarai confide in her, woman to woman? Did she treat her with kindness? Or, as this incident suggests, did she treat her like an object to be used for her own purposes? If there had been any kindness in their relationship, it ended here. Sarai considered Hagar only as a means to her own ends, not as a person to be seen and valued as a child of God. Giving birth to children was the most common cause of death for women in this era, but Sarai was willing for Hagar to risk her life to bear a baby for her.

Running Away When Life Gets to Be Too Much
(Genesis 16:4–16)

Hagar could never become a full wife; at best, she could be a concubine, never equal to her mistress. She could take out her frustrations by getting in some subtle jabs aimed at her mistress's most sensitive feelings, however. The *Tanakh* correctly translates Genesis 16:4: "her mistress was lowered in her esteem." Her own bulging tummy broadcast the success of Sarai's stratagem, but it also did something else. It silently proclaimed, "I am a complete woman, and you are not." Hagar may not have been all that silent. An indiscreet word dropped here and there could only make Sarai feel more inadequate. She suffered from the law of unintended consequences. Sarai wanted to build herself up through Hagar's offspring, but the result when Hagar became pregnant was that Sarai's self-esteem plummeted even further and her psychological misery became greater than before. Her pent-up feelings finally boiled over into rage. She complained to her husband that her slave was putting on airs and disrespecting her. Hagar had taken her place in her husband's bed and had proven her worth as a woman by becoming the mother of her husband's child, while Sarai felt dowdy, old, and empty. Her wounded pride and resentment caused her to lash out at Abram for doing what she herself had suggested.

She whined to Abram, "Hagar treats me with contempt! Don't you see it? Can't you hear that tone in her voice? Can't you see the way she sashays around me with her belly sticking out? Can't you see the way she mocks me now? Why don't you do something about this? She needs to be put in her place, but all you do is go around patting her belly and cooing. I gave her to you to embrace, but there is entirely too much embracing going on! That is *my* child—our child, but she acts like it's hers!"

Abram, with all the sensitivity of an armadillo, says, "She's your slave-girl. She is in your power. Do with her what you will. It was all your idea, after all. Don't come bothering me about it. It was your brilliant plan; you fix it." No help for Sarai or for Hagar was going to come from this quarter. So Sarai took out her feelings of inadequacy and anger on Hagar, who was, she reasoned, *just* a slave-girl. She was only a baby incubator, and an entirely too uppity one that needed to be put in its place. The Bible tells us simply, "Sarai dealt harshly with her" (Gen. 16:6), or better, "she afflicted her" (authors' translation). It is the same verb that is used to describe the afflictions that the Hebrews would suffer during their slavery days in Egypt (Exod. 1:11–12; Deut. 26:6). It is left to our imagination to guess exactly what Sarai did. Did she engage in the psychological warfare of emotional abuse by insulting and demeaning her? Did she give her dirty, menial tasks to do? Did she beat her? We do not know. Whatever she did, it was bad enough to make Hagar run away pregnant *into the wilderness*. Her name means "flight," and she lived up to it.

Running away pregnant with nowhere to go was a desperate act, and Hagar's "nowhere" led into the wilderness. Where in such a place did she think that she would find refuge? What could she do? No one treated runaway slaves with kindness. It was an ironic twist; she was trying to escape her oppressive slavery in the Promised Land and get back home to the freedom that Egypt represented for her. We can feel her despair when she comes to a spring of water, tired, thirsty, and hungry, with a baby kicking in her womb. At her wit's end and with no strength to go any farther, she collapsed in a heap.

An angel of the Lord came to her and asked her what was already known in divine headquarters, "Hagar, slave-girl of Sarai, where have you come from and where are you going?" (Gen. 16:8). By addressing her as "Hagar, slave-girl of Sarai" it is obvious that the angel knew the situation, and it was an unpleasant reminder of her predicament. She was a runaway slave. The question was not asked because the angel was uninformed. It was intended to get Hagar to rethink her situation and what she was doing. Was it the best plan? It is still the question we ponder today when we find ourselves collapsed in the wilderness: Where have we come from, and where are we going? Hagar had only a partial answer. "I am running away from my mistress Sarai" (Gen 16:8). She might have added, "That is where I am coming from. Where I am going—well, that's up in the air right now. Where can I go?

I have no more strength to go anywhere. I have no family to go to who will take me in."

We who find slavery so abhorrent today might hope that the angel of the Lord would have helped her escape from her slavery. The angel might have said to her, "You're right. You have been treated inhumanely, and I will help you to get out of this." But the angel did not say that and did not guide her to the nearest stop on the underground railway that would speed her way to freedom. Instead, the angel said, "Return to your mistress, and submit to her" (Gen. 16:9). We may think this command terribly harsh and uncaring. Aren't angels supposed to help us? Why doesn't the angel whisk her across the barren wilderness and set her up back home in Egypt as her own mistress? The angel did announce that God had heeded her affliction (Gen. 16:11). Heeding it is one thing; fixing it is another. God did not offer her what we would consider a decent answer to her need, just the hard word to go back and submit. Hagar was afflicted by Sarai, and she was told to put herself back under that affliction.

This word is hardly the word of liberation we have come to expect from God. Katharine Doob Sakenfeld notes that this is no liberator God, but that returning will allow Hagar and her child to survive (2003, 21). Sometimes, all God helps us to do is to survive. Divine intervention does not always deliver us from our troubles but simply helps us just to get by. We expect from God an experience of grace, renewal, freedom, love, comfort, strength, meaning, and hope. We want more during the times when, as Anne Lamott says, "We're very much alone and it's all scary and annoying and it smells like dirty feet and the most you can hope for is that periodically someone will offer a hand or a rag or a tiny word of encouragement just when you are going under" (1994, 200). This word to Hagar hardly sounds like a word of encouragement or the offer of a helping hand. God seems to have thrown her back into the dirty clothes hamper. But it is better back there with Sarai and Abram than out in the wilderness with the vultures circling overhead. Sometimes, survival may be the best we can expect. God does not offer a way out but a way through and the promise that God will go with us along the way. But the way leads along stony, foggy paths. In a situation that was too much for her, she learned that with the God who sees her, nothing is too much for her.

Foolishly, Hagar had tried to make her escape with no thought of what she might need for such a journey, or where she would go. Alone in the wilderness, she had put her life and the life of her baby at risk. The angel of the Lord came to her and rescued her. On the run from her mistress, she met the God who most often shows up during dire personal crises to bring assurance of divine care and mercy. It was an experience of grace for her just to know that someone had noticed what was happening to her—and that someone was God, no less. Hagar had an encounter with God, just like Abram. She named the Lord who spoke to her, "El-roi," which seems to mean "the God who sees," for she said, "Have I really seen God and remained alive after seeing him?" (Gen. 16:13) or "I have now seen the One who sees me," that is, "the One who looks after me" (Gen. 16:13, NIV). She was surprised that there would be any deity who would even notice her misery, let alone show favor to her in this desolate place.

Sarai had not seen her as a person but as an object. As a slave, Hagar was supposed to be invisible, a nonperson. When Sarai saw Hagar's growing belly, it led only to abuse, not acceptance. But God saw Hagar, and in her mind this divine attention—that God would attend to a slave-girl—was a miracle in itself. Therefore, she obeyed and did as the angel commanded. She went back to her mistress. We can cope with a lot if we know we are not alone, if we trust that God sees, and sees us in our miserable plight. God was working in the life of Hagar. Her path was a difficult one, but the angel encouraged her to see that she could do it with God's hand on her. That made all the difference.

Following the path God has for us does not mean that the journey will be one of ease and ready fulfillment. Only in fairy tales does everyone live happily ever after, and not always even there. In the story of Sleeping Beauty, part two, as the Grimm brothers told it, the prince's mother was an ogress. Beauty's mother-in-law devoured the children that a nurse futilely tried to hide, and she tried to kill Beauty in a pit of snakes. The world is filled with dangers and with evil. How does one cope? Anne Lamott has said, "Everything is going to be Okay but we do not know exactly what Okay might look like" (1994, 87). Grace allows us to receive what comes in life with gratitude. God helps us to accept that the "Okay" in life embraces it all, the good and the bad, the joyful and the painful, the holy and the not-so-holy. Grace from God gives us the strength to get through it all and survive, and lets us leave the future in God's hands. The way God accomplishes the divine plan may seem to be a bit like a Rube Goldberg setup, an extremely intricate contraption designed to effect a relatively simple result. All we can do is hang on for the ride, trusting that it will all work out in the end.

The word of God to go back and submit also came with a promise to Hagar. She would bear a son, to be called Ishmael. As God promised Abram many descendants, so God promised Hagar descendants too numerous to count (Gen. 16:10). The predictions about her son, however, were not very encouraging: "He shall be a wild ass of a man, with his hand against everyone, and everyone's hand against him; and he shall live at odds with all his kin" (Gen. 16:12). This boy was going to be a handful. Hagar was going to have many more afflictions for God to heed.

What could she do? The son to be born was hers and yet not hers. How could she discipline him? How could she ensure that he would be loved by Sarai and well provided for by Abram? She must stand by and watch someone else parent him—two octogenarians hardly up to chasing toddlers around, and who had demonstrated that they were not the strongest when it came to family life skills.

The Bible does not tell us how Hagar was received when she arrived back home. It is safe to say that she was probably not smothered with embraces, a new robe, or a ring, and celebrated with the slaughtering of the fattened calf to prepare for a welcome-home party, as the prodigal son in Jesus's parable was. She was still a slave, but she was back home and safe, for now. The time came and she bore Abram's son, and he named him Ishmael, which means "God hears" (Gen. 16:15). Abram must have listened to the voice of Hagar on this one and given him the name she suggested, the name God had told her. He may have interpreted it all to mean that God hears the cries for a son and has now answered. But this was not the fulfillment of the promise.

Fulfilled Promises (Genesis 17)

More than a decade went by, and Abram, at age ninety-nine, received another word from God: to circumcise all the males of his household as a sign of his covenant with God. With this covenant, God changed his name from Abram to Abraham and changed Sarai's name to Sarah (Gen. 17:5, 15). Because she was not part of this promise, Hagar stayed Hagar. Her thirteen-year-old Ishmael was circumcised as God commanded, but a new threat to Hagar's and her son's precarious security arose. God reminded Abraham of the promise uttered long ago that Sarah would bear a son, and now God was ready to deliver on it. Abraham saw that this would complicate his home life considerably, and so he tried to tell God that he had already worked out for himself the question of an heir. "Everything is reasonably okay. Ishmael is a fine boy. He will do. Let Ishmael enjoy your special favor. That will be good enough!" (Gen. 17:18, authors' paraphrase). But "good enough" was not the plan. God said, "Your wife Sarah shall bear you a son, and you shall name him Isaac. I will establish my covenant with him as an everlasting covenant for his offspring after him. As for Ishmael," God said, "I have heard you; I will bless him and make him fruitful and exceedingly numerous; he shall be the father of twelve princes, and I will make him a great nation" (Gen. 17:20). "The covenant, however, I will establish with your son Isaac, whom Sarah will bear around this time next year" (Gen. 17:21, authors' paraphrase).

It had been twenty-five years since God spoke the initial promise to Abraham. He was now nearly a hundred, and Sarah was nearly ninety. It had been a difficult twenty-five years, with painful detours along the way. A final word came from the Lord, this time via three divine visitors who showed up mysteriously. Although Sarah stayed in the tent, preparing the food for the men and being modest, her ears were tuned in to the conversation outside between Abraham and the visitors. The Lord spoke, the story says, presumably in the voice of one of the men. "I will surely return to you about this time next year, and Sarah your wife will have a son" (Gen. 18:10, NIV). When Sarah overheard this astounding news, for the first time she no longer had to believe her husband's word about God's promise; she heard it with her own ears. It gave her a laugh. She tried as best she could to stifle it and be discreet. It was not a belly laugh, but rather a silent chuckle as she reflected on her situation, "I am dried up and worn out, and my antique husband is in even worse shape" (Gen. 18:12, authors' paraphrase). But this was the Lord, and the Lord heard her silent laughter and her thoughts. Speaking to Abraham rather than to her, the Lord said, "Why did Sarah laugh? . . . Is anything too wonderful for the LORD?" (Gen. 18:13–14). The Lord saw and heard Sarah, as he had Hagar, even in her silent laughter and doubt. Frightened, Sarah lied, saying, "I did not laugh." Perhaps she was being legalistic, thinking that because her laughter was silent, it did not count. God countered, "Oh, yes, you did laugh" (Gen. 18:15). It was a gentle reprimand. It had been a long journey for Sarah.

Indeed, Sarah became pregnant, and at their ages it was a miracle. We can imagine that they had already made plans to enter the Rose of Sharon retirement home, and here Sarah was pregnant. She bore a son, and Abraham gave him the name Isaac, which means "laughter." The name referred back to the time when God broke the news that Sarah, who was already "past the age of childbearing," would bear a son. Abraham fell over with laughter (Gen. 17:17–19), later echoed by Sarah (18:12). And no wonder. It had taken almost a lifetime of waiting, but Sarah was vindicated, and so was God as one who makes and keeps promises. She exulted, "God has brought laughter for me; everyone who hears will laugh with me" (Gen. 21:6). One wonders if the joke was not on her, giving birth when she was old enough to use a walker to push a baby stroller. But laughter seems to be an appropriate response when humans receive by faith God's great work.

Ishmael was a teenager and thus finding his own identity when his stepbrother Isaac was born. Trouble brewed when the two sons, Ishmael and Isaac, tangled later. The Hebrew is not clear whether Ishmael mocked or somehow threatened his younger half-brother. A jealous sibling rivalry probably stirred in Ishmael's heart. He had been the only child, showered with the blessings of *three* parents, believed to be the bearer of the promise, and positioned to inherit his father's considerable wealth as the firstborn son. But with the birth of Isaac, he suddenly became superfluous and was demoted to the son of a slave. Now, with the fulfillment of the promise in Isaac, Ishmael's future in this family seemed to be shattered. Moreover, Ishmael had some behavioral changes he needed to make—he was a wild one. Hagar had been warned about him; he would be getting into trouble with just about everyone.

At the first sign of the brewing storm, Sarah went to Abraham and ordered him to kick out this slave woman with her son. No longer did she consider Ishmael her own son, as she had when she hatched the plan and wheedled Abraham into having a child by Hagar. Sarah treated this tender-aged boy as an object to be discarded, as something no longer useful. She wanted him purged from the family. "We do not need them anymore. Isaac has now come, and he should inherit everything alone. Hagar and Ishmael are just trouble. Get rid of them."

Abraham was fond of Ishmael and distressed at this new demand, but he pondered the matter. God helped him with the decision by telling him to do as Sarah told him. "As for the son of the slave woman," God said, "I will make a nation of him also, because he is your offspring" (Gen. 21:13). So we are back to the beginning of the Hagar story. Abraham sent them off into the wilderness of Beer-sheba with as much water and food as they could carry. What words passed between Abraham and Hagar when she and Ishmael were thrown out, the Bible does not record. She was no longer an escaped slave but now a free woman. Nevertheless, she faced a long, arduous trek through the wilderness to get back home to Egypt.

Apparently, they could not carry enough to get them all the way to wherever they were going. Abraham had given them what they could carry, but evidently none of the herd of pack animals and treasure, gifts from the Pharaoh that included Hagar herself, that he had left Egypt with so long ago. The water ran out, and Hagar was once again in a desperate situation in the wilderness, with death imminent. She sat Ishmael under one of the bushes because she could not stand to see him suffer and die. She then lay down and began to sob bitterly. This time, God heard the voice of the boy crying, and the angel of the Lord called down from heaven with what appeared to be another ridiculous question: "What troubles you, Hagar?" (Gen. 21:17). Hagar could have said, "What do you think troubles me? Don't you know what has happened to me and my son? You are supposed to be the God who sees me. We are about to die out here in this wilderness. A fat lot of good it did to go back and submit to my mistress, only to be thrown out and have to watch my son die of thirst."

The angel calmed her, saying what angels usually say in dire circumstances, "Do not be afraid. God has heard the cry of your boy, and he will not forsake you. As promised, God will make a great nation of him" (authors' paraphrase). Hagar had not been able to see through her tears. So God opened her eyes, and she saw a well. There was enough water for them to drink their fill and make it to the next rest stop. It turned out that God was with this boy as well. He would grow up, settle down in the wilderness, and become an expert marksman with the bow. His mom even got him a nice wife from the land of Egypt. One wonders if God is not also an expert bowman, as Oswald Chambers said about God's handling of our lives: "A saint's life is in the hands of God as a bow and arrow in the hands of an archer. God is aiming at something the saint cannot see; he stretches and strains, and every now and again the saint says: 'I cannot stand any more.' But God does not heed; he goes on stretching until his purpose is in sight, then he lets fly. We are here for God's designs, not for our own" (1963, May 8).

Ishmael had not been included in the covenant God made with Abraham, but he was not excluded from God's blessing. It was the blessing that all humanity lives under (Gen. 1:28). Just as the progeny from Isaac would become a great nation of twelve tribes (Gen. 49:1–27), so the progeny from Ishmael would form a great nation of twelve rulers (Gen. 25:13–15).

The fulfillment of the promised son to Sarah and Abraham resulted, too, in the fulfillment of God's promise to Hagar, to watch over her. She was back in the wilderness, and in desperate straits, but this time, God had a different word for her. Here was water enough for her to go on—not back. The time of submission was over. She still had to journey through the wilderness, but this time it was as a free woman, with the provisions of God to see her through. She was free of the jealousies and rivalries of Sarah, freed from slavery, free to be the mother of Ishmael and all who would come after, and not just a borrowed womb. Sometimes we seem to come around to the same place we have been before, only to find paths that previously were not open to us. Perhaps they were hidden in a fog that is now lifting just enough to see a new way.

Abraham and Sarah had to learn to stop trying to depend on their inadequate, human resources to control their future and instead to depend on God to handle the matter. It may have taken so long for God to deliver on the promise because God was not trying to teach them something new but trying to get them to unlearn something old, which takes much longer. They had to unlearn their reliance on their own feeble self-sufficiency and put their trust in the sufficiency of God. Maybe that is what God meant when God told Abraham, "Walk before me and be blameless" (Gen. 17:1, NIV).

Does this mean that we should sit and wait on God and do nothing? Is the lesson here that faith is passive? Do we say to friends who are suffering in awful circumstances to "wait on God," or "our time is not God's time"? No, we *walk* by faith; we do not *sit* by faith. We take one step after another, after another, doing our best to steer toward the fog that is not only the future, but God's future. Abraham and Sarah must have believed the promise and so been intimate with one another after the angels' visitation, perhaps with laughter, with one saying to the other, "How many times do you think we have made love in these eighty years together?" Isaac was not born by an immaculate conception. His old parents had made love in response to God's promise. This, too, was an act of faith. It contrasted with their earlier actions, which really were acts that doubted God's faithfulness. Earlier, they tried to get what God had promised—a future and a future with children—by abusing others: Abraham by selling Sarah to the pharaoh, and Sarah by forcing Hagar to become Abraham's concubine. This time, they got it right. Out of laughter and lovemaking came Isaac.

If the life of this family were an airplane flight, it would not be a calm passage. They were bounced around pretty good, and at some points it looked like they might stall and crash, but they had a safe landing. I (David) was on a puddle-jumper flight in a small plane, and the person sitting across the aisle looked quite nervous as we were taxiing to take off. It was her first flight on one of these "dinky" planes, as she called them. "Are they safe?" she inquired. In one of my impish moods, I said, "Sure they are safe! I have gone down twice in planes just like this and walked away both times." After a puzzled pause, she began to laugh and then relax. She was even more puzzled when I told her that I taught in a seminary and was flying out to preach at a church. Why would a preacher make stupid jokes like this? I said that I trusted the people who made the plane, and I trusted the mechanics and the pilots. There will be a safe landing. The same is true in life even when our lives seem muddled and the future seems bleak. We can trust the one who made us, watches over us, and hears our wails of despair and our silent sighs of hopelessness, and we can let this one pilot our lives until touchdown. But we have to take the step of getting on the plane.

When Hagar cried out in the wilderness when her life was desolate, she received divine consolation from the God watching over her. She got what she needed—fresh words from God and just enough vision to see her through her troubles. Edmonia Lewis's sculpture of Hagar resides in the Smithsonian American Art Museum. Details about Lewis's life (1845–1911) are hazy, but she was of mixed racial heritage—her father was an African American, and her mother was a Native American—and she suffered from discrimination in the United States and later landed in Rome, where she was free to work as an artist. She became the first African American and Native American female sculptor of renown. She seems to have identified with Hagar, also an African, believing that she symbolized all women who have suffered and struggled. Her sculpture captures Hagar's sense of hope as she looks off into the horizon with her hands clasped together in a firm resolve. That sense of hope associated with Hagar may be why an organization that develops programs aimed at transforming the lives of the poor and disadvantaged women in Cambodia by educating them and giving them the skills to be productive and self-sufficient picked the name "The Hagar Project." They apparently chose this name because they saw a connection between Cambodia's homeless women and children and the story of Hagar and her son. On their website, they write: "Taken advantage of when young, many become mothers at an early age, then are despised and cast out. They are vulnerable to further abuse and often end up living on city streets with both emotional and physical scars and little hope for the future" (www.Hagarproject.org). It is an apt name for a project that seeks to rescue the vulnerable. The Hagar story offers hope, a hope in a God who hears the cries of those who are afflicted and distressed and whose future seems blanketed in fog. Sarah's story reveals that one should never give up on God. Hagar's story helps us see that God's care and presence penetrate every human condition—even that of a hapless and hopeless runaway slave-girl.

The stories that follow recount the experiences of those in the Bible who experienced distress, trauma, and meltdowns—much like the lives of so many families today. All of us have felt the discouragement and doubt of Sarah and the sense of abandonment and despair of Hagar at one time and another in our lives. The stories of Hagar and Sarah set the stage for reading them in the light of God's care and grace. Life does not always go the way we think we have been promised. If we go through the storms, the fog, and the bumpy rides trusting in God's guidance and loving one another rather than hurting one another, it will help us get through it all with a spirit of hope.

Hope versus hopelessness is captured in the poem "On the Way to Work" by Stephen Dunn (1989). The poem begins with him driving to work and spotting a bumper sticker proclaiming: "Life is a b---h. And then you die." He wondered why people wanted to be known "by one glib or earnest thing" expressed in a sound-byte-sized bumper sticker. He also wondered whether the woman driving the car that bore this message thought it was a joke or what she wanted to communicate to the folks who saw it or what she wanted from them. He had his own public answer: "New Hope for the Dead." If he'd had those words on a bumper sticker plastered on his car, he would have wanted to slip his car in front of hers and slow down so that she would see it. Maybe, he fantasized, they would strike up a friendship or at least a conversation if they ever connected. But she turned off in a different direction. The poem concludes:

> She didn't follow, not in this
> b---h of a life.
> And I had so much to tell her
> before we die.

This is the message of the stories retold in this book: New Hope for the Dead—and also for the despairing, downtrodden, deflated, defeated, downgraded, and despised.

Some people are graced by life. They grew up in a "good" home; they have "good" looks; they have "good" things come their way. For others, life is anything but gracious and sublime. Being graced by life, however, does not save anyone. The only thing that is important is to experience being graced by God. You know then that when your life is messed up there is hope. It does not solely depend on you to unmess it or to try to earn your worth.

2

Leah's Story

When Your Spouse Loves Another and You Feel Unloved and Left Out

I (David) had just started to teach from the Gospel of Matthew in a seminary class. We were looking at the strange sorority of women included in the genealogy of Jesus (Matt. 1:1–17)—Tamar, Rahab, Ruth, the wife of Uriah. I pointed out that the stories behind these names, except perhaps Ruth, are hardly the moral high spots of the Old Testament. One student remarked, "If I were to include women in the genealogy, I would not have included these women. I would have singled out Sarah, Rebekah, and Rachel." I said, "No! Not Rachel but Leah!" I must have said it a bit too sharply, because I got a startled look from the student and the class. The look said, "Leah? You've got to be kidding!"

Leah went through most of her life getting quite similar reactions to her presence. Rachel was the favored one, the one who received all the attention, both growing up in her father's home and as Jacob's beloved first choice for a wife. Leah was unloved and left out. I heard someone recently pray to the God of Abraham and Sarah, Isaac and Rebekah, and Jacob and Rachel. It was a politically correct prayer, because it included the wives along with the husbands. But it left out Leah. She seems to have been one of those ill-fated persons destined to be overlooked.

It may have begun the day her baby sister Rachel was born and everybody oohed and aahed over her. Well-meaning but insensitive people remarked to her mom and dad in the hearing of Leah, "Isn't Rachel beautiful; you must be so proud." Later they would say to Rachel, "How much like your beautiful mother you are!" Then they would spot Leah hanging back out of the way, become embarrassed, and try to cover themselves without blatantly lying: "Oh, Leah dear! What a pretty dress." Or perhaps, worse, they would say, "Aren't you excited to have such a pretty little sister!" Leah's name means "wearied," which seems appropriate. Some say it could mean "cow." Rachel means "ewe." Rachel was a cute little lamb. Leah was Elsie the cow. Next to Rachel, perhaps she felt like a cow. Who can ever live up to the image of the ideal, desirable female of cultural fantasy, then or now? We live in a world that values people who are slim over those who are more rounded, those whose hair will best take the currently popular styles, and those with clear skin and the most fashionable hues. Who has not stood in front of a mirror and been discouraged by the reflection they see there?

When I (Diana) was in elementary school, my sister and I played Tarzan in the backyard. Being the bossy one, at least with my little sister, I would take the role of Tarzan and cast her as Cheetah the monkey. She was not even allowed to be Jane. Like many sisters, we jockeyed for position not only in our games but also in our relationship with our parents. Sometimes I won; sometimes she did. We were different enough in age that we did not compete for boyfriends or find ourselves in the same peer groups. Our parents found ways to communicate their love for both of us as unique individuals, each of us with lovable qualities that brought them joy.

Parents of rival siblings face the formidable task of helping each claim the beauty and gifts God has given them and learn to honor those gifts in the self and in the other as well. Evidently, Leah and Rachel's parents were not sensitive to the struggles of their daughters, to Leah's desperate need for affirmation that she, too, was a child precious and beautiful and worthy of God's purposes. Worse, their father, Laban, just wanted to get Leah off his hands and married by hook or by crook.

Love at First Sight (Genesis 27–29:13)

The situation did not improve for Leah when Cousin Jacob showed up without warning. Whether Leah and Rachel knew the details of the saga that caused him to land suddenly in their lives, we do not know. He, like Rachel, was a youngest sibling, but by just a few minutes behind his twin brother, and his contention with his brother had some tense moments. Jacob was on the lam, trying to escape the wrath of his elder brother, Esau. Jacob had bamboozled him out of his birthright as the firstborn. He coaxed a famished Esau to exchange his birthright for a bowl of red stew. He then had the gall to deceive his half-blind father, Isaac, into thinking he was Esau by putting goat skins on his arms so that when Isaac reached to touch him to bless him, he would feel like hairy Esau, not like the smooth-skinned Jacob. Consequently, Isaac bestowed on Jacob all the blessings that should have gone to Esau as the firstborn. Jacob had stolen every privilege of being the firstborn from his brother. He had it all, leaving Esau with nothing except his rage.

Rebekah, Jacob and Esau's mother, had always favored Jacob and had helped him to plot the deception. What kind of mother feeds the rivalry between her sons, planting ideas in the mind of one of how to steal blessing from the other? There was no trust here, no safety that home is a place where others care for one's well-being. For Jacob, home had become too dangerous to stay, because of what he had done at his mother's encouragement. Esau was ready to kill him. For Esau, home had become a place where even his own mother betrayed him by helping his brother rob him of his father's blessing for the future.

Husband Isaac must have been furious with Rebekah when he learned that she had helped Isaac to deceive him. It was probably not the first time that she had used the children as pawns in the marital relationship. This family had apparently been divided into camps for a long time, Esau and his father quietly warring with Rebekah and Jacob. Now the war had broken out openly, with the very real possibility of violence to avenge deceit and dishonor. Rebekah knew that if Jacob was to survive unharmed, he would have to leave, so she shipped him off to her brother Laban. Perhaps there Jacob might even find a suitable wife. Favoritism, jealousy, selfishness, deceit, betrayal, division, murderous anger—these are the family legacies that Jacob carried with him as he looked for his Uncle Laban.

Poisonous rivalry seemed to plague this family for generation after generation. Isaac's mother, Sarah, had championed his cause over that of Ishmael, Abraham's son by her handmaid Hagar, splitting the family. Hagar and Ishmael were thrown out and almost perished in the desert trying to make it to a sanctuary where they could start life anew. A generation later, Jacob was fleeing the family just as Hagar and Ishmael had been forced to do.

When he made his escape and pulled into the rest stop near Uncle Laban's spread, he spotted the beautiful Rachel, Laban's daughter, coming to water her sheep at the well. In the Old Testament, the well was *the* place to check out the available young women—much as the mall functions today. Perhaps the teenagers then said to one another on a boring weekend night, "Let's go down and cruise the well." At the well, Jacob faced down a bunch of rough-and-tumble shepherds who were harassing this lovely young woman trying to water her sheep. When he turned to look at her, he was mesmerized. He kissed her and wept—from joy, and perhaps from relief that escape from home might result in finding love. He then fulfilled that innate male need to impress women by picking up the huge stone covering the well and giving it a toss so that Rachel could water her sheep. The contrasting descriptions of Esau as a cunning hunter, a man of the field, and Jacob as a homebody (Gen. 25:27) may lead one to imagine that Jacob was a weak mama's boy. This well episode spoils that picture. The well cover normally took several men to budge, but Jacob had no trouble lifting it on his own. Rachel must have been suitably impressed by this feat of strength and his rescuing her from the shepherds' harassment. At least, she did not discourage him as she took him to meet her father, his Uncle Laban.

Two Tricksters Doing Battle—Meet Uncle Laban (Genesis 29:13–20)

Uncle Laban was thrilled to meet his sister's boy. "Ah, my dear boy, my flesh and bone! Are you here for a long visit?

Just because you are my kinsman, you needn't work for me
for nothing. Tell you what I'll do, boy, I will let you work here
for me, and you name the wage." Jacob had not mentioned
anything about working, but love does something funny to
one's thinking, and his wily business acumen that finagled
his brother into giving up his birthright for some stew failed
him. He offered seven years of service for the hand of Laban's
younger daughter, Rachel. Laban could hardly conceal his
glee. He had just been offered seven years of free labor and
the chance to keep his wealth in the family with a nephew
as his son-in-law.

But what about the older sister, Leah? Daughters were supposed to be married according to birth order. Leah apparently
did not strike Jacob's fancy. The Bible says that Rachel was
shapely and beautiful, as it says of Sarah and Rebekah, only
with more emphasis. It may explain why Jacob fell in love
with her at first sight. Leah, it says, had "weak eyes" (Gen.
29:18, RSV). The word describing her eyes was also used to
describe something that was frail (Gen. 33:13), gentle (Deut.
28:54, 56; Gen. 18:7), tender (Isa. 47:1; Ezek. 17:22), and soft
(Prov. 15:1; 25:15). Translations adopt different interpreta-
tions. The legend that she wept her eyelashes away in dread
anticipation of having to marry her hairy first cousin Esau is
pure fancy. Whatever this adjective is meant to describe, it
is clear that Jacob was not smitten with her the way he was
with Rachel. She did not have the same appeal.

Apparently, there were no other suitors asking for Leah's
hand in marriage and no suitable prospects during the seven
years that followed. She was still unmarried at the end of
the seven years. Laban wanted her married and may have
been frustrated that he could find no one to take her. Our
heart goes out to the unwanted Leah. No man wanted her
as wife, and her father wanted her married off. What better

candidate than Jacob, since it would mean that the family's wealth would stay in the clan?

So, Laban hatched a scheme. He would trick Jacob into taking Leah. Did Leah want to be married so badly that she agreed to her father's deceitful plot? Was she so convinced that no one would ever want her that the only way to marriage was for someone to be tricked into taking her? Possibly, she always did whatever her father told her to do, whether her heart was in it or not. Later, after the sad marriage to Jacob, her desperate ploys to get some of his affection and respect, even if it was only a token, suggests that she really did want to have a husband to love her and to love. The text is sparse and tempts readers to add their own embroidery. Could it be that during those seven years of labor in Laban's household, Leah had peeked from behind the curtains at Jacob toiling away on her dad's farm, and her attraction and affection for him grew?

The Wedding Night Switch (Genesis 29:21–27)

Uncle Laban made the switch of Leah for Rachel on the wedding night under the cloak of darkness, when the marriage was to be consummated. Jacob, who had tricked his blind father, now was deceived himself. The trickster gets tricked. One wonders how Laban and Leah pulled off such a ruse—and why Rachel allowed it to happen. She too was a victim in this deceitful family plot. Jacob had lived with them for seven years; surely he would know the difference between Rachel, his heart's love, and Leah her sister, even in the dark under the covers! The Bible does not explain how it worked. The bride wore a veil, which was taken off in the darkness of the bridal chamber, but the Hebrew for wedding feast basically means "drinking party." After seven

53

years of labor to win his beloved, too much celebratory wine may have befuddled Jacob's mind. Combined with his desire finally to consummate this relationship, somehow Jacob was fooled. The scripture is very discreet and void of details. It simply says, "When morning came, it was Leah!" (Gen. 29:25).

Since Esau was done in by the shrewd and calculating Jacob, who took advantage of his wolfish appetites to get him to sell his birthright for a bowl of soup, it may be poetic justice that Jacob was done in by his own appetites—his feasting, drinking, and eager sexual groping. But justice for whom? Certainly it was not justice for Leah, who apparently craved a husband so desperately that she hoped against hope that when morning came, Jacob would forget all about Rachel and love her.

The Bible does not record Jacob's first reaction at morning's light, but we can imagine it. When the sun rises, Leah's temporary happiness evaporates like the mist. The Bible also does not record Leah's reaction to Jacob's dismay. Again, we can guess. What must it have done to Leah's soul to know that her husband did not love her, did not want her? What must it have done to her soul to look into the eyes of her husband and know that he loved another, her sister? She had imagined that he might just favor her with a little affection, that for the first time in her life she would be wanted by someone, but she could see it in his eyes. There was no affection—only bitter disappointment and anger at her presence. We've all had those experiences when somebody says: "Oh, it's just you!" or, "Oh no, not you!" It can stay with us a long time. Leah had just married that experience. She looked at a life stretching before her with a man who did not want her and had never wanted her. Perhaps she had hoped the night beneath the covers would change his mind and make him love her. If she met his needs, gave to him, he would want her. But she was wrong.

Jacob cried foul. "You deceived me!" he yelled at his uncle, now his father-in-law (Gen. 29:25). Families so often repeat over and over patterns of hurt and betrayal. They must make concerted attempts to live out the love and grace that God intends to characterize families. Jacob's "You deceived me!" echoed Isaac's cry when he realized Jacob fooled him: "I have been deceived!" (Gen. 27:36, authors' paraphrase). Jacob had now become the fool. If Leah heard the conflict between her father and her husband echoing through the family compound, neither of them wanting her, she must have been heartsick. Her husband felt betrayed by her very presence.

Jacob was squaring off against an uncle who was also a master cheater; deceiving and betraying seemed to run rampant in this family. Laban tried to humor Jacob. "Didn't you know that it is the custom here never to marry the younger daughter before the older? I am so sorry. It's the firstborn's birthright to be married first. We honor such things like that around these parts." Mentioning the firstborn harked back to Jacob supplanting his brother Esau's rights as the firstborn, a deft little taunt. As Jacob's mom schemed to steal rights from her elder son for her younger son, Laban schemed to ensure the rights of his elder daughter to the disadvantage of his younger one. Turnabout is fair play, one might think. Jacob had met his match in Laban. The two would spend twenty years as father-in-law and son-in-law trying to outfox each other.

Laban's plotting continued, and it laid the groundwork for everyone's suffering. "Listen, boy," Laban said, "Do I have a deal for you—two for one! Wait until the bridal week is over—just seven more days—and I will give you Rachel." He may have mumbled the extra condition, "That is, if you put in seven more years of work for me." He sounded like a TV peddler hawking his store's big furniture sale: "Just call me crazy, but I need to move the merchandise. You can't beat a bargain like this!" Both his daughters were simply pawns and their father the pawnbroker, wrangling a deal. Neither daughter much appreciated her father's conniving schemes that ignored her feelings. Did Leah even know that her father would also give Rachel to be the wife of her husband? When Jacob decided it was time to bail out and return home, he gave a long-winded speech to his wives about being cheated by their father and receiving a vision from God, thinking he needed to cajole and convince them to abandon their home (Gen. 31:1–13). The two sisters, however, needed no convincing. They were in total agreement. Their father was a jerk who had bartered them away. They were glad to leave this swindler who made his own daughters feel like foreigners (Gen. 31:14).

Leah's Pain (Genesis 29:28–30)

Seven days, and you can have Rachel. Rachel was still the chosen one. What a honeymoon week it must have been for Leah, knowing that her husband could not wait for it to be over. Then, in the second week of her marriage, she had to watch the new lovebirds coo and cuddle in the blush of romance fulfilled. Undoubtedly, she no longer shared a bed with her husband; she had been supplanted by Rachel. Perhaps she had hoped that somehow the previous week when she had him to herself would be so wonderful that Jacob would fall in love with her as he had Rachel. It was not to be. It must have dawned on her quickly that she was trapped now in a marriage that destined her to compete with her sister for her husband's affection, with all the cards stacked against her. The gaping void in her life that may have caused her to agree to the midnight swap in the first place would only grow larger and larger.

Most of us can remember times in our lives when we were not the one chosen. It can cause emotional scars that never seem to heal. Or, perhaps, we fell out of favor with people we loved and became also-rans in their lives when they moved on to someone else who seemed more glittery and alluring. Leah faced that most of her life, but she faithfully performed her marital duties for an ungrateful husband whose real affections were elsewhere.

God saw that she was unloved, the Bible tells us. After all, she had Laban for a father, Rachel for a sister, and Jacob for a husband. The ominous word of the Lord to Rebekah about the twins in her womb, "the elder shall serve the younger" (Gen. 25:23) seemed to be true in Laban's family with Leah and Rachel. Leah was forced out of the firstborn role to take a back seat to her sister who was Jacob's beloved. The sibling rivalry of their childhood escalated with both married to the same husband. They scrambled to get his time, attention, love, and approval and may even have tried to manipulate him to ignore the other wife. Leah started out a distant second but refused to give up without a fight. What kept her continuing to try to win Jacob's affection when she knew he loved another?

Many of us know how it feels to be unloved, unappreciated. For some, it is a fleeting experience; for others, those feelings last a lifetime. Sometimes we think we might do something to make others love us, respect us, appreciate us. "If I do this," we tell ourselves, "they will finally appreciate me for what I do." It is often a pathetic hope. Evidently, Jacob continued to visit her bed on occasion. For Leah, the only reward in her marriage was birthing babies—bouncing baby boys. She named her firstborn son Reuben, which is a play on the Hebrew words for "see" and "son." The ancient Hebrews did not choose a name because they liked its ring or they wanted to carry on a family name; names were often snapshots that give us a glimpse into the joys and heartaches of the parents. With the name Reuben, Leah shouted, "See, a son!" She announced, "Because the LORD has looked on my affliction; surely now my husband will love me" (Gen. 29:32). Her most desperate longing was to be loved. She wanted her husband to look on her and to see her with new eyes, to see some value in her. She wanted him to feel delighted and grateful for her.

She was to be disappointed yet again; Jacob's attitude toward her appeared not to have changed. He was still sleeping with her, but he found no delight in her. She was not loved. She had a second son and named him Simeon, meaning, "Because the LORD has heard that I am hated" (Gen. 29:33). *Hated* conveys in English "to loathe or despise," but in the text it is a Hebraic idiom that simply means "to love less," "to be indifferent to." By this point in the story, we are not surprised and may wonder why Leah expected anything more. After all, her husband had been tricked into marrying her. Knowing that, however, did not ease the pain for Leah or curb her yearning to be loved or her determination to count for something in his eyes. She still longed for a crumb of love, some confirmation, if only a token, that she mattered. She may have had "weak" eyes, but she had a strong spirit. She kept trying. Why? What was it that drove her? It was a hopeless situation, but she was not without hope. Maybe in her cries to God, she trusted that God would not only see that she was hated but do something to help.

It may seem that Leah was overly self-centered, but it was a product of her pain and low self-image, which was reinforced by her husband's disregard for her. Son number three was conceived, and she named him Levi ("joined"). Perhaps she thought the third time would be the charm, because she said: "Now this time my husband will be joined [attached] to me, because I have borne him three sons" (Gen. 29:34). She had given up on "love." If only her husband would be attached to her.

We are attached to family, even when we may feel no love there. For example, children who have been abused and neglected by parents and removed to live in a safer place are still emotionally attached to their parents. These children may readily admit that their parents do not seem to love them, but given a choice, they will go home to them, because those parents are "home," no matter how inadequate they are or how they have failed in the past. Leah's home was with Jacob, even if he did not love her.

She had given up on trying to become first in his heart; all she asked was to be family with him. Again Leah was to be disappointed. But with the birth of her fourth son, Leah sees her situation with new eyes. She named this fourth son Judah ("praise"). We can see her pain in the previous names. This name represented a shift. She said, "This time I will praise the LORD" (Gen. 29:35). Forget Rachel and Jacob! Forget trying to earn Jacob's love! Forget even trying to get the scraps of Jacob's affection! Having babies will not repair a loveless union. Jacob was not going to change. So she exulted, "I will praise the Lord!" Is it a revelation? Did she realize that the Lord is more apt to remember her devotion and service and to be more appreciative than her husband? She no longer needed what she could not have from Jacob in order to experience joy.

The slew of babies provided only momentary triumphs for Leah. She was only being serviced by a dutiful husband. After Judah, the pregnancies stopped, and her torment worsened. She began to understand better what her barren sister Rachel was suffering while she birthed son after son. Even being the number one wife did not protect Rachel from feelings of insecurity. As Leah may have clenched her fists in rage at being the one unloved, Rachel gritted her teeth that her sister was bearing all these babies—and baby boys, to boot—from the rare intimate interludes she had with Jacob. The shame of not giving Jacob children must have eaten away at Rachel's soul.

Women have a natural desire to conceive, to bear, to nurse, and to protect, but in Rachel and Leah's culture, the number of children, particularly sons, that a married woman bore determined her value as a wife and a person. However much Jacob had loved Rachel for her beauty—and he may have pointed that out once or twice in the clumsy way that husbands do—she believed in her heart that she was failing him as a wife and failing as a woman. In this family, so characterized by self-interest, jealousies, betrayal, and deceit, could Rachel trust that Jacob's love would continue in the face of her humiliation? Might she lose her place in the family? He had sold out his own brother; might he sell her out, too? She could not trust her sister or her husband, those closest to her.

No one in this family seemed to know anything much about unconditional love. Rachel had received everything she wanted in life because of her looks, and now that was not working. She too must have felt desperate and alone. Leah could very well have said to her: "Welcome to my world." But it was not a family in which one could easily lay bare one's deepest insecurities and vulnerabilities. It has been said that shared grief can knit hearts closer together than happiness can, but the two sisters' bitter rivalry kept them from sharing with each other their common pain. Neither offered to the other a wing of comfort for her to nestle under and feel understood, cared for, and safe. They built walls instead of bridges, and they became imprisoned in their loneliness. Living in this family was like living in quicksand. Each one was struggling alone to keep from going under, and their flailing about just seemed to make them sink deeper.

Consequently, Rachel tried to shore up her position with Jacob by giving him her maidservant Bilhah as a consort. For two sisters to be wives of the same husband and to have their maidservants also involved sexually with him at the wives' instigation may strike us today as providing all of the ingredients for an unhealthy family, to say the least. If these folks were living today, they would be prime prospects for making the rounds of the sleazy afternoon talk shows. The story does get steamier with the concubine rivalry, and Jacob does not seem to have had the moral backbone to recognize this as a bad plan and a recipe for family disaster. He just goes along. We know from the Sarah and Abraham story that the surrogate motherhood route only adds to the family turmoil. For Jacob, it is far worse. We have a family of wives and concubines all competing to whelp the most sons.

Giving Bilhah to Jacob seemed to do the trick for Rachel in the baby competition arena. First came Dan, and Rachel's triumphant declaration: "Vindication! God has judged me, heard my cry, and given me a son" (authors' paraphrase) Then came Naphtali and the boast: "With mighty wrestlings I have wrestled with my sister, and have prevailed" (Gen. 30:8, authors' paraphrase). It was a different kind of wrestling than Jacob had with the angel at the river Jabbok (Gen. 32:25). It was the tug-of-war of interpersonal relationships as each grappled with the other to earn the affection and attention of a man who does not seem to us to be worth it.

Leah did not sit idly by in this contest, and she gave Jacob her maidservant Zilpah. One wonders what these maidservants thought about all this, but the Bible does not say. They did not even get to name their own children. Along came another boy, whom Leah named Gad, which supposedly means "What luck!" And then Asher was born, whose name suggests, "Women call me blessed," and Leah basically declares, "Happy days are here again!" The sisters waged an escalating contest to produce the most babies, and Rachel was losing. Rachel became convinced that the secret of her sister's fertility lay in the magical properties of phallic mandrake roots, fancied to be an aphrodisiac.

Mandrake love potions were thought to increase sexual desire (see Song of Sol. 7:13). Leah's boy Reuben found mandrakes in the field and brought them to his mother, and Rachel wanted some for herself. When asked by her sister for some mandrakes, Leah did not try to hide the pain she had been feeling all these years: "Is it a small matter that you have taken away my husband? Would you take away my son's mandrakes also?" (Gen. 30:15). Though she never enjoyed his affection, she had convinced herself that her husband had been stolen from her by her sister.

The only way for Leah to have some value in this family was to continue to produce children. Leah had become so desperate that she stooped to bartering with her sister simply to spend time with Jacob. Rachel offered to take a batch of mandrakes in trade for allowing Leah to spend a night with their husband. Leah knew that Jacob would never love her for herself; she had to hire his attention. When Jacob trudged in from the field, Leah greeted him with what must have been bitter words: "I have hired you with the mandrakes of my son." No reaction from Jacob is recorded. He spent another dutiful night with her.

Leah conceived again and bore a fifth son, this time proclaiming triumphantly, "God has given me my hire because

I gave my maid to my husband" (Gen. 30:18). So she named this boy Issachar. Still hoping for some respect, she bore him a sixth son. "God has endowed me with a good dowry; now my husband will honor me, because I have borne him six sons"; so she named him Zebulun (Gen. 30:20). Finally, she gave birth to a daughter, Dinah. The pendulum seemed to have swung back in her favor. Yet, at the end of the day, all she had was honor and respect for her baby-producing capabilities. She had asked God for children, and children had been granted. At the same time, Rachel gave birth to two sons of her own. Joseph was her firstborn. She had received the answer to her own desperate plea: "Give me children or I shall die!" (Gen. 30:1). But in this fierce competition with her sister for honor, one son was not enough. When she gave her newborn his name, she said, "May the LORD add to me another son!" (Gen. 30:24). Another son, Benjamin, came along, but she died giving birth to him. She got her wish, and it killed her.

Where is God in all this rivalry and deceit? Does all this marital competition and jealousy fit somehow with God's purposes? Jacob's family was supposed to be the family of the promise, the fruit of God's covenant with Abraham. All these children were born into and grew up in a war zone of rivalry, envy, and desperate trickery. One is tempted to ask, does God really want this bunch for a chosen people? Imagining the edginess of their home life, we can certainly understand how generation after generation went through one scrape after another with God, with their neighbors, and with one another. It is probably not surprising that Leah's sons would eventually sell their brother Joseph, the son of Rachel and spoiled by their father, into slavery to some peddlers on their way to Egypt.

The law later would wisely forbid taking one's wife's sister as a rival wife, "uncovering her nakedness while her sister is still alive" (Lev. 18:18). That law came too late for Leah. On the other hand, these kinds of family dynamics can character-ize family relationships that seem perfectly normal even by today's standards. It doesn't take a situation where a husband is married to two sisters for jealousy, rivalry, deceit, and self-centeredness to cripple a family. These dynamics carry over from one generation to the next, just as Rebekah and Isaac's patterns of deceit and division with sons Esau and Jacob shaped the families of their sons and grandchildren.

Into Egypt and the Next Generation (Genesis 46:8–27)

The offspring from Leah and Rachel are tallied in Genesis 46:8–27. From Leah came a total of thirty-three, counting sons, a daughter and grandsons, and from Zilpah her maidservant came sixteen, for a grand total of forty-nine. From Rachel came fourteen descendants, and from Bilhah her maidservant came seven, for a total of twenty-one. For those keeping score, which they undoubtedly were, it was a rout for Leah.

In some congregations, they still give flowers to the woman with the most children and grandchildren present on Mother's Day. One can imagine that every single Mother's Day, Leah would have won the flowers. But was she happy? A horrible pattern was repeating itself before her eyes. Just as Jacob had loved Rachel best, now he was clearly showing his love for Rachel's firstborn, Joseph, far more than for her own brood of strapping boys. And so, the jealousy and rivalry of their mothers characterized the relationships between their sons by Jacob. Some of us have an inkling of what this must have felt like for Leah. It is one thing to suffer ourselves. It is even more painful to watch our children suffer injustice. How did Leah bear the injustice she had lived with her whole life now being visited on her boys? Where did she find the courage to keep on?

The rivalry among the stepbrothers erupted in violence. Joseph was sold into slavery by his stepbrothers when he vainly flaunted his father's favor. After near-death scrapes, Joseph worked his way into a position of power in Egypt, and all of Jacob's offspring eventually tromped off to live under Joseph's patronage.

The God Who Watches over the Unloved

Leah appealed to God in the naming of her sons and, over time, those names changed in their tenor. What does her story say to us centuries later? Who is Leah to us?

All of us know what it is like to have our service taken for granted by others—spouses, children, employers, or coworkers. What thanks do we get for years of faithful devotion? Sometimes, precious little. We may even wonder if God ever notices us. Injustice abounds. Lives of service and commitment go unappreciated. I (David) taught at an institution for years, where I made regular use of the library. One day, it dawned on me that several weeks had passed since I had seen a kind librarian who had worked there for a long time. I finally asked the person checking out my books, "Where is Miss Smith? I haven't seen her for a while."

"Oh, she retired," she replied.

"Retired!" I blurted out. "Why didn't anyone get notified? Why weren't the faculty told? I have been checking out books from her for twenty-five years. No one on the faculty got to say thanks or even goodbye."

"Oh, they had a farewell meal for her," she said.

"Where?"

"In the student cafeteria."

When administrators retired, the institution gave them cars and condos. Yet someone who gave her whole life to the school in unsung service leaves unannounced, with only a going-away dinner in the student cafeteria. Her name was not Leah, but it could have been.

Leah teaches us that God cares for the unloved, but it does not necessarily mean that they will be loved by the ones here on earth from whom they are so desperate to receive love. It does not mean that they will ever be fully appreciated. In the movie *The Divine Secrets of the Ya-Ya Sisterhood*, based on Rebecca Wells's novel of that name and her *Little Altars Everywhere*, the daughter in the story, Siddalee Walker, describes her childhood in an interview in *Time* magazine as "dual-edged," which raises the hackles of her self-centered, overly sensitive mother. The mother breaks off the relationship with her daughter, which causes the Ya-Ya sisterhood, a group of the mother's lifelong friends, to go into emergency action to repair the damage between mother and daughter. The movie fills in the story with flashbacks of the mother's own painful childhood, a courtship that ends in her handsome fiancé's death in World War II, and her marriage to a cotton farmer. Her husband was second choice and second best. The rocky relationship teetered on the brink of disaster when the mother was involuntarily committed for six months to a psychiatric hospital after imbibing a toxic mixture of drugs and alcohol. Her second-choice husband toughed out this seemingly unhappy marriage and counsels his daughter on how to relate to her mom: "It wasn't always bad, honey. Do what I do. Think about the good times. Let that be what sticks with you." When asked why he stayed with his wife all these years, he responds that it was either play second fiddle or not play in the band at all. His daughter thinks he is some kind of saint and asks, "Daddy? Did you get loved enough?" He responds, "What's enough?"

Leah stuck it out all those years because she had no other options. Did she get enough love from her husband? What is enough? Yet there is more to come in the long story of the family of Jacob, Rachel, and Leah. Rachel, her rival wife and sister, died giving birth to Benjamin, and Jacob was devastated. He buried her on the road to Bethlehem and built a pillar for her there (Gen. 35:19–20). Did the relationship between Leah and Jacob change after that, or was it already changing? We learn from Genesis 49:29–31 that years later, Jacob buried Leah in a place of honor next to Abraham and Sarah and Isaac and Rebekah. When he neared the end of his long life and began making his own burial arrangements, he told his sons not to bury him in Egypt, where he had come to be with Joseph and his brothers. Instead, he told them to take his bones back home to the land of promise: "There Abraham and his wife Sarah were buried; there Isaac and his wife Rebekah were buried; and there I buried Leah" (Gen. 49:31). Interesting. He does not ask to be buried next to Rachel, whom he favored most of his life, but next to Leah, his first wife, the one he never wanted to marry in the first place. If we could ask her, Leah might say, "Too little, too late." But maybe not. Perhaps after all those years of birthing babies and competition and after the death of Rachel, Jacob and Leah found that indeed they had become family for each other, flawed though that family was. Maybe Jacob finally "saw" Leah as his life partner. Jacob joined himself to her in death, the answer to her plea so long before when she had named her third son Levi ("joined"). It is then not inappropriate to pray to the God of Abraham and Sarah, Isaac and Rebekah, Jacob and Leah.

When we look back at this story from our vantage point, we can see even more the mysterious ways of God. Somehow in God's wonderful wisdom, Leah was the one to bear most of Jacob's children. She bore his firstborn son. She bore Levi, who would be the father of the priestly line in Israel. She bore

Judah, who would be the father of the royal line. Through Judah would come King David and, eventually through this line, a child named Jesus. Leah was a significant link in God's plan.

Who is to say that even difficult family relationships might not be a part of God's plan to redeem us and future generations? Perhaps Jacob learned what true love was all about in those years with Leah. Maybe Leah learned that you can give your best even when you are thought to be second best. In wedding ceremonies, the minister should not ask, "John, *do* you love Abby?" But "John, *will* you love Abby?" Using the future tense recognizes that love is not a feeling that you have or don't have at any given moment. It is an act of the will. It is something you decide to do. Something you promise to do, something you act upon. Even when love might go unappreciated, who is to know what God will do with it? Who knows how it will all end? The future, after all, belongs entirely to God. When Leah named her fourth son Judah, "God be praised," she had no idea what lay in the future. She may have had her doubts and asked herself, "If God is in control, why is my life such a mess?"

Even though the crazy ways of this family carry from one generation to the next, we see a shift in the sons of Leah and Rachel. Yes, there was jealousy and treachery. Leah's boys had sold Joseph, Rachel's boy, to traders headed for Egypt and into a life of slavery. But later, when the sons of Leah, starving from famine, go to Egypt to seek food from the household of the king, there is a wonderful story of finding themselves at the mercy of this betrayed brother—and there finding forgiveness. Through the grace of God, the working of the Spirit in the imperfect places, change happens. Families can be places of redemption rather than places of wounding, places of reconciliation rather than places of betrayal. Who would have ever imagined that happening in this family?

God doesn't work through mandrakes or magic, and God's ways are mysterious to everyone, even those who have regular and intimate dealings with God. This is the God who takes a wild-eyed, fierce persecutor of Christians and turns him into an apostle of good news. This is the God who takes mockery and death on the cross and turns it into the good news of the resurrection. This is the God who can take our lives, broken as they are and chock-full of disappointments, and turn them into good news for others.

3

Dinah's Story

The Horror of Rape and
Living through Family Shame

Genesis 34 and Judges 19

The Bible recounts sordid stories of rape—the rape of Dinah, and her brothers' savage revenge (Genesis 34); the gang rape of the concubine and her dismemberment (Judges 19); the rape of Tamar by her half-brother Amnon, and her brother's fierce retaliation (2 Samuel 13). What is the point of these stories? These skeletons in the histories of biblical families are not hidden away in closets, never to be mentioned, but the gruesome details are laid bare for all the generations to read. They certainly are not read much in church and are rarely mentioned. The subject of rape is hardly ideal content for a

Sunday school lesson, and when a brave pastor does preach from one of these texts, people are likely to squirm in their pews. They may not want their children to hear them and may wonder what the pastor was thinking bringing R-rated stories into the church. Nevertheless, these stories need to be told. If we do not read and tell these stories, these women are forgotten, implying that their lives were unimportant and that the violence they endured had no meaning. They were precious to the heart of God, and not to remember and retell their stories "would signify that their lives were of little consequence and their deaths of no significance" (de Groot van Houten 1997, 15). Moreover, these stories need to be retold because the experiences of these women in the Bible have happened to so many women today. A survey found that 44 percent of women report having experienced at least one attempted or completed rape (Russell 1984, 15). These biblical stories can help us find the meaning in current life experiences.

Rape happens to both men and women, but because most victims are girls and women, and because the stories in the Bible are of women, we will use female references. Our intent is not to ignore or diminish the violence that men and boys who are abused have experienced.

Rape is a profound violation of another person. It violates the other's will and assaults her personhood and her autonomy. The rapist reduces the victim to an object to be used for gratification of some desire without regard for the victim's well-being or for the victim's status as a human being created in God's image. Rape can be an expression of overwhelming lust, but more commonly it is an expression of rage intended to humiliate and demean another human being.

The trauma of the experience often keeps a victim from talking about what happened to her. She frequently suffers from posttraumatic stress (C. P. Flynn 1990; Rothschild 2004). Keeping silent, however, can be disastrous for her. She may try to pretend that it did not happen, or that it was not as bad as it really was. The experience remains a wordless cloud of feelings, unprocessed emotions, and inarticulate memories and fears that haunt her waking and sleeping life. Instead of telling her story, she may attempt to contain the damage from her experience by refusing to think about it or talk about it, putting it in a mental box tightly lidded, locking it, and throwing away the mental key. This approach almost never works. It is like trying to store toxic chemicals in a cardboard box. The experiences leak out and poison the whole system. In unspoken ways that a victim may only dimly understand, she lives her life with the buried memories working stealthily to inflict damage on her soul and to erode her health with various symptoms. She remains a victim rather than becoming a survivor. She knows that because of her silence, moreover, the perpetrator is not confronted and can go on to victimize others.

Telling the stories of her experiences gives her a way to begin to understand, manage, and relieve the emotional wound so that it doesn't control her life. If the victim does tell others what happened, however, she risks exposing herself to people who do not understand the dynamics of rape and having her character assassinated by community gossip and possibly even by the media. Even her family and closest friends may wonder what she did that contributed to her victimization. Was she in the wrong place at the wrong time? Was she asking for it? How was she dressed? Did she look at him when she should have avoided any eye contact? They may even wonder if she swiveled her hips in some seductive way. Others may have their doubts. Was it consensual, and now she has changed her mind? Telling what happened can often cause her to feel assaulted and defiled all over again, as she dredges up the experience buried in the dark recesses of her soul. Reliving the experience as she tells the story can deepen the trauma rather than lessen its effects if she does not feel safe, accepted, and supported by those who hear her.

A victim needs to be able to tell her story in a family or community that listens compassionately, reassuring her that she did not cause her victimization, and offering hope that she will survive it because they will be there to support and love her. She needs understanding and the willingness of others to walk with her through a long, dark, seemingly endless valley where the shadow of death seems to hover everywhere. In the despair that follows rape, particularly for those victims who have no support, suicide is common.

One of the ways that we can become compassionate communities and families is to hear Bible stories of tragedy and victimization that make us feel uncomfortable. They do not lend themselves to a popular interpretation of Romans 8:28 that "all things work together for good to them that love God" (KJV). There is no obvious redemptive message from these stories, but hearing them together in a community that seeks to understand these biblical women's experiences may help the victims in our midst see a way through the dark valley. It may be difficult to find in these stories meaning that God has for all of us, but the word of God has a powerful and surprising way of breaking through our seemingly impenetrable defenses and our unyielding despair, to bring light and redemption.

Anne Lamott, for example, tells of her fitful conversion experience in her book *Traveling Mercies*. She was raised to be an atheist by her parents and was caught up in the culture of drugs and promiscuous sex. Her conversion began in her sophomore year of college. A professor made Søren Kierkegaard's *Fear and*

Trembling assigned reading. What struck her like a lightning bolt was Kierkegaard's account of the sacrifice of Isaac. She says that she left class believing that there was a God, and it made no sense at all. She said *it made no sense* that what brought her to the conviction that God exists was this story of a God who asked his beloved Abraham to sacrifice the child he loved more than life itself (Lamott 1999, 27–28). For most Christians, this story of God's request that Abraham sacrifice his long-awaited son Isaac on an altar would be lumped together with the long list of names in 1 and 2 Chronicles as one of the last passages they would ever use to win someone to faith in God. For Anne Lamott, however, it had an amazing power. Some stories, like the rape of Dinah, seem to make no sense and are muffled in the church. We may be muzzling a story that may allow God in some mysterious way to help those who also have become victims of violence. It may be simply that hearing the story presented in a way that attends to Dinah's experience may communicate that someone in the church understands and cares and that God understands and cares.

We have a responsibility to help victims become survivors, to seek justice for them, to be sure their stories are not forgotten and that our communities are ones of protection and healing, not further victimization. Retelling the story of the violence done to someone like Dinah breaks the silence, shows belief in her, and shares her outrage. Silence only protects the perpetrator and allows him to continue to spread evil; it does not protect her or help her (Fortune 1995). It simply allows the evil to fester.

Dinah Ventures Out (Genesis 33:18–34:3)

After Leah had given birth to six sons, Dinah came along almost as an afterthought, as it is recorded in Genesis 30:21:

"Afterwards she bore a daughter, and named her Dinah." She was the seventh child, an auspicious number according to biblical reckoning. We know almost nothing else about her. The Bible recounts the reasons each of her brothers is given his name, but no such explanation is given for Dinah's name, perhaps because she is not a head of one of the twelve tribes, as her brothers were. Her sisters go unnamed, and we do not even know how many there were. It reminds us that in this age girls did not count. We know about Dinah only because of her bitter fate. Hers is the only story of a daughter of one of the patriarchs, and it is not a pretty one.

It all began when Jacob had settled down outside of Shechem after twenty years in exile on Paddan Aram. He failed to fulfill his vow at Bethel that he would return to that place, build an altar, and worship God there (Gen. 28:18–21). Instead, on the way back home, he pulled up short, bought land, and built an altar outside of Shechem, hoping to coexist peacefully with the locals.

Everything seemed to be going along fine, until Dinah decided to go out and check out the new neighborhood. She left the home camp to visit the daughters of the land (Gen. 34:1). She may have had no idea how imprudent her foray all alone into a strange city was. To venture alone into a city was dangerous, particularly a city of Canaanites, who were regarded rather dismally in the Bible as a people steeped in vice. Apparently, she went out without permission and without a companion or chaperone. Perhaps she was lonely and felt that she had been stuck for too long with her indifferent father and only her rough-and-tumble brothers as companions. Who can stay all day in a tent? Her mother was dead, and she needed female company. This new community offered the prospect of finding friends, and perhaps some adventure and a welcome change of scenery. Her own family life had long been dominated by the extended battle between her mother, Leah, and her stepmother, Rachel, for Jacob's attention and their competitive trying to produce the most baby boys. Who wouldn't want to escape the tension and loneliness that must have characterized life for a daughter in this household? Maybe she inherited that roaming gene from her great-grandfather Abraham that had been passed down to her own father, Jacob. Not only was Jacob's family a tense place, but they had been on the move as nomads, traipsing from one community to another. Regardless of what drove her to embark on her adventure, Dinah naively did not realize the danger she was creating for herself. She was still a minor child, just a girl. Where was Jacob? Had no one warned her against going out alone? Had Daddy ignored the admonishment to parents to know where your children are at all times and to know who is with them? Was she as unloved and neglected by Jacob as Leah had been?

The Bible tells us only that Dinah went out to see and to be seen, as teenagers today might go to the mall or the local hangout. She was exploitable, and her family's lack of prestige in this foreign society left her unprotected. She wanted to be seen, and Shechem, son of Hamor, saw her. He also lusted after her. Initially, she may have been dazzled by this man who gave her the attention that she did not receive at home, but she was also intimidated by him. He was a prince, equivalent to the star quarterback on the football team and the dashing prom king. As a prince, he was probably used to having his way with women, getting whatever he wanted, or getting away with whatever he wanted. The Bible states it simply and graphically. It does not use any language that implies consent. Shechem took advantage of Dinah's friendless situation and grabbed her and raped her. She could expect no help from the villagers, had she cried out.

Some interpret what he did as simply an ancient and customary way of acquiring a wife. The Hebrew verbs make clear, however, that she was seized and taken against her will. Even though the text says that afterward he loved her and spoke tenderly to her, his act was rape, not lovemaking. He was a sexual predator who raped, and then he spoke tenderly to her to excuse his behavior. It is like the BTK ("bind, torture, kill") serial killer arrested in Wichita, Kansas, in 2005, who testified that he showed "compassion" to one of his victims by giving her a pillow to rest her head on as she lay dying.

Shechem basically attempted to cover what he had done by doing what may have been customary in his day and what the Law of Moses later would require. According to the law set down in Exodus 22:16, "When a man seduces a virgin who is not engaged to be married, and lies with her, he shall give the bride-price for her and make her his wife." If the father refuses, he has to pay the going rate in the bride price for virgins (Exod. 22:17). It is also declared in Deuteronomy 22:28–29:

> If a man meets a virgin who is not engaged, and seizes her and lies with her, and they are caught in the act, the man who lay with her shall give fifty shekels of silver to the young woman's father, and she shall become his wife. Because he violated her he shall not be permitted to divorce her as long as he lives.

The law implicitly assumed that the raped virgin was now damaged goods, and it was best for her to marry the assailant. Who else would want to marry her? As with a new car damaged on the car lot by a hailstorm, who would want to pay full price? The requirement was a form of punishment on the man, because he could never divorce her—you did this to her, now you are stuck with her. This law was written not to encourage this approach to marriage, but rather as a deterrent to rape. It took an act of irresponsibility done with thoughtless disregard for the personhood of the other and made the perpetrator responsible for the rest of the woman's life.

Not only was the law designed to prevent rape, if rape did occur, it gave the victim some security. She might be damaged goods from the male standpoint that placed a premium on virginity for marriage eligibility, but she now belonged to the man who had done violence to her. This approach fell far short of justice for the victim and did not completely remedy her predicament. She was sentenced to life with a man who was a rapist, a violent man. She had no choice in the matter. Who would choose to be married till death do us part to someone who had begun the relationship with such violence?

Dinah was not a teenage daughter attracted to the worst sort of boy as a way to upset and to get the attention of her parents. The text says nothing about her attraction to Shechem. Even if she was interested in him, that does not absolve him of responsibility for what he did. The author makes it clear that her feelings were not at issue, because they are never mentioned. Whatever she felt or did, she was not responsible. There is no excuse for his violation of her—not how he felt about her, not whether or not she was attracted to him, not anything she did.

Any idea of female complicity in sexual attacks is a male myth. She may have been trapped after innocently accepting an invitation to a private place where he could have his will. Like women who are victims of date rape, she may have thought she was safe with him and so let down her guard. He may have set her up to trust him, as a means of isolating her. Her naiveté does not make her responsible for what happened to her; neither would any possible attraction on her part. She may have been like many rape victims, frozen by fear. Many women are encouraged and conditioned to be passive and warned that resistance can result in serious injury or worse. The lack of resistance may convince a rapist that he has her consent.

We hear no word from Dinah. She is silent throughout the entire story. Like so many victims, she was probably in shock, emotionally swamped by the trauma and her own sense of guilt for having been "so stupid." Victims often blame themselves for what happened to them, and others reinforce that guilt by piling it on with questions like, "Why did you go out alone? Why did you go there with him? Why didn't you fight him off and escape?"

Like most abusers, Shechem alternated abuse with words of love. He raped her, and then he spoke tenderly to her, saying that he loved her. We can imagine the scene. "Sweetheart, it will never happen again. I love you. Trust me. I was just so overcome with love for you, I couldn't help it." The trauma of violence cannot be healed with dismissive flattery. Words and deeds of affection do not excuse or diminish the abuse he had inflicted. Even if he had felt some form of love for her, his words were manipulative, a way to keep her in his power. The words may have sounded loving, but they were part of a cycle to restore her trust, to keep her in his power, so that he could abuse her again. They were simply ploys to keep her docile and ensnared in his web.

Dinah Is Held Captive While the Fathers Negotiate (Genesis 34:4–12)

Shechem told his father, Hamor, "Get me this girl to be my wife." He found her pleasing and wanted to possess her more permanently. It may be that he thought that his behavior would be justified by marrying her or that he simply wanted to keep her around. From his cultural perspective, he may have viewed the rape and kidnapping as an accepted way to marry someone outside the clan. It is a vestige of the old caveman days as imagined by cartoonists; the caveman conks a woman on the head and drags her by her ponytail back to his cave. This male perspective is an effective strategy for downplaying the violence and abuse inherent in what Shechem did.

Shechem acted as though nothing unusual or disturbing had happened. He thought he could negotiate a marriage by force, giving no thought to Dinah's personhood or what she might have wanted. Violent people often feel entitled and almost always fail to realize the impact of their actions on others. And if they were to understand the impact, they probably would not care. Shechem approached the matter of marriage to Dinah, a human being he had abused, like a horse trader. He wanted his father to pay anything to acquire her for him. His father's name, Hamor, means "donkey" in translation. It is possible that the donkey was an animal sacred to the city, but the name also is a slap at his character and the character of his son. They were worse than donkeys. Perhaps, in fact, identifying them with donkeys is an insult to those creatures, known for their stubbornness but not for their violence. Our son, who is a farmer and pastor, has a fearless and stubborn little guard donkey that bravely chases off any packs of dogs that threaten the chickens—protecting, not harming. Hamor and Shechem are both stubborn and violent.

Hamor winked at his son's indiscretion and agreed to make a bargain with Jacob for the girl. When he and Jacob met, he mentioned nothing about rape—his son's violent abuse appears to have been accepted or ignored by Hamor—boys will be boys. This was a culture that did not fear God, where rape was at home, and where women were bought and sold like chattel.

Hamor viewed Dinah only as an opportunity for creating political bonds with these seemingly affluent outsiders. This marriage offer from Shechem to Jacob was pitched as a means to forge an alliance between the two groups and to merge them. It was a political business deal. Hamor and Son, Inc., offered free trade, property sales, and a free exchange of daughters as brides for Jacob and Sons, Inc., as part of the deal for Dinah (Gen. 34:9–10, 21).

While the two fathers carried on their negotiations, Shechem held Dinah in custody as a hostage. What must she have felt? Did she wonder why her father did not come to rescue her? Did she wonder if her family cared what happened to her? Did she sense the looming disaster and blame herself? Did she wish that she were dead? Did she hate the one who violated her with a searing hatred, praying for avenging furies to retaliate? Or did she succumb to the so-called Stockholm syndrome, in which a hostage begins to empathize with his or her captors?

Only in the last few decades has it been recognized that rape can happen even in marriage. Just because two people are married does not give one the right violently to assault the other, nor does it make rape anything less than what it is—a violation and degradation of the other's body and soul. The rapist uses sex as a weapon to humiliate and dominate. Rape by a marital partner is more deeply traumatizing, moreover, than violence at the hands of a stranger, because it undermines a woman's ability to trust those closest to her and destroys her basic confidence in herself. She has to live with her attacker, not just a frightening memory (Yllo and LeClerc 1988). Research shows that the closer the relationship between the victim and the rapist, the more violent the assault tends to be. In other words, marital rape tends to be more vicious and violent than rape by a stranger. It is the very opposite of lovemaking (Pagelow 1988). It is quite possible that the rape of Dinah occurred repeatedly as she was held hostage, as well as after her marriage to Shechem.

Why didn't Dinah attempt to escape? We often ask the same question today if a women is being abused by her partner: why doesn't she just leave? Again, research shows that violent men often threaten to kill their partners if they try to leave, and they mean it. If she had tried to leave, he might well have killed her. She may not have been physically restrained, but she was clapped in psychological irons. It should come as no surprise that a high number of women in this situation commit suicide or attempt to kill their abusers, when they believe it is the only means to escape or to protect themselves and their children. Research also shows that the majority of American women convicted of killing their mates had previously been beaten by them. Women charged in the death of a violent mate do not have criminal records; yet less than twenty years ago, they were frequently sentenced to longer prison terms than were male murderers (Browne 1988).

Dinah's sense of abandonment and despair was probably compounded by Jacob's astounding passivity. His daughter had been raped and now was captive in the household of her rapist, but Jacob did nothing. He seemed indifferent to his daughter's trauma. Jacob's willingness to bargain trivialized her degradation. Was it because he did not care about any of Leah's children, who were never the apple of his eye? But what can we expect from a father whose daughter is raped? What can he do? He also would have been in a state of shock. Jacob had a responsibility to protect his children; his daughter's rape was a proof of his failure, at least in his own mind. Perhaps he wanted to pretend it did not happen.

Bury it. Work a deal and move on. Jacob had always been willing to haggle; wheeling and dealing and deceit characterized his whole life. He had stolen his brother's birthright and his father's blessing. He had bargained for his own wives and had fleeced their father out of a great deal of his wealth. It all seemed to come back on his head; and now, perhaps, he was paralyzed, not knowing what to do.

Hamor sought to assuage any anger or desire for revenge for what had happened by appealing to Jacob's acquisitive instincts. "Let's work a deal. No price is too high," he told Jacob. They could work out an advantageous trade arrangement and throw in some real estate to sweeten the package. How could Jacob turn down a bargain like this? Perhaps Jacob resigned himself to what had happened to Dinah. Let bygones be bygones. He might as well see if he could make some profit from it. Jacob was ready for the political and economic alliance, and, who knows, perhaps even a religious alliance might be in the works down the road. Dinah was violated and raped, taken captive, and now abandoned and sold off by her father. But what compensation would ever be enough? Even when rapists today are punished with prison terms, the victim and her family are left with the bitter truth that no length of prison term compensates for what has happened. The violation continues to haunt them.

The Brothers Protect Their Reputation (Genesis 34:13–31)

When Jacob's sons, Dinah's brothers by Leah, got wind of what had happened, they had a very different reaction. As far as they were concerned, there would be no concord with these donkeys, no matter how much they were willing to pay out. They were seething with rage over what had been done to their sister and bitter that their father was willing to give in so easily and sell her out to these louts (Gen. 34:7). They talked their father into adding another condition to the settlement that he was forging with Hamor. If Shechem wanted to marry a nice Jewish girl like Dinah, then he would have to be circumcised. And if they wanted to do business with Jacob's clan, then all the men in their tribe would have to become circumcised as well. Then they would allow Shechem to keep Dinah as his wife, or at least that was what they promised. Circumcision was the distinguishing mark of Israel and a sign of the covenant with the God of Abraham (Genesis 17), and it was probably sold to Hamor as all part of the merger of the two families. Hamor's family would take on the sign of Jacob's family. The brothers were plotting to use this sign as a ruse, part of their plot to wreak vengeance on the perpetrator of the violence against their sister. No one asked Dinah what she thought would be best for her—she was still a captive in the household of the rapist. No one seemed to care about what she needed. Also, no one asked God about what to do. God's voice is also absent from this story.

Shechem was smitten by lust for her and was willing to go to great measures to take possession of her. His father, Hamor, and Dinah's father, Jacob, negotiated because they wanted to increase their prosperity. Simeon and Levi, Dinah's brothers, wanted revenge to restore the family's honor. What Dinah wanted we are not told. Where was God in all of this?

Shechem must have really wanted Dinah—or to be allied with her wealthy father—to be pleased with conditions that required circumcision. And his father must have been in the custom of spoiling his son rotten to think such surgery for the whole clan was a good idea. That they talked the other men in town into agreeing to this plan is cause for amazement. They must have had astounding persuasive powers. Shechem and his father dangled the carrot of the economic windfall that would come their way if all the men would go along. The combination of brides and business prospects and whatever power Shechem and his father wielded cinched the deal. They had no idea what was coming.

Levi and Simeon belonged to Jacob's family of liars and tricksters. They took Lamech's boast, "If Cain is avenged sevenfold, truly Lamech seventy-sevenfold" (Gen. 4:24), to the ultimate degree. They resorted to the law of the desert: Do not appear weak; avenge family honor. Their sister had been victimized because they were perceived as weak, and they intended for this never to happen again. The family's honor was at stake. If their do-nothing father was going to let bygones be bygones, they would have to take matters into their own hands.

Dinah's brothers were livid because their father was treating this whole matter as if their sister were a prostitute. When her father, always the shrewd wheeler-dealer, listened to an offer from Shechem to purchase her—"Put the marriage present and gift as high as you like, and I will give whatever you ask me" (Gen. 34:12)—indeed he was treating her like a prostitute. In effect, it meant that her sexual services were for sale, and he was her pimp, picking up the cash she earned from this sexual encounter. Jacob's former indifference to his daughter's welfare was compounded now by his greed: "Everything will be fine by me if I get compensated properly." This attitude outraged the sons of Leah. Their sister was no prostitute; they would not stand idly by and allow her to be treated like one; and Shechem would pay for this indignity. Dinah's personal tragedy was about to spread like waves from a landslide into a lake, swamping everyone in both communities. Shechem had turned sexual union, which was supposed to be a sacred, generative partnership between a man and a woman, into a brazen act of violence and degradation. The annihilation of his whole world would be the result.

When the Shechemites were recuperating from the painful circumcision surgery and temporarily incapacitated, Dinah's brothers Simeon and Levi turned into a two-man army and treacherously decimated the lot of them with a surgical strike of a different nature. In a sneak attack, they massacred every male, liberated their sister, and plundered the city. They took flocks, herds, donkeys, and whatever loot they could lay their hands on and hauled it all away. Their sister had been defiled by one man, but they took all of his clansmen's wives and little ones in merciless revenge. How many dead in the city, how many women captured and presumed raped in acts of domination, the Bible does not say. The brothers believed that might made right. The blood from the rape of a virgin was avenged by the blood of hundreds.

Jacob was aghast at the news of the mass murder. But his concern was only self-centered, just as his lack of response to the news of Dinah's rape had been. When he finally speaks in this story, Jacob expresses only worry about his own well-being:

> You've made my name stink to high heaven among the people here, these Canaanites and Perizzites. If they decided to gang up on us and attack, as few as we are we wouldn't stand a chance; they'd wipe me and my people right off the map. (Gen. 34:30, *The Message*)

Jacob expressed no concern about the outrage done to his daughter or the injustice of his sons' deadly sneak attack against untold numbers of innocents. He cared only about the potential consequences to himself. He worried that his name would now become mud throughout the whole region. Who would do business with him now? Other communities might even muster an army, march against him, and wipe out his whole family in retaliation, if they had any alliances with Hamor. Years later, when Jacob lay on his deathbed and gathered his sons around him to give them his last will and testament, what Simeon and Levi had done still stuck in his craw. He cursed their anger and cruelty that had wrought such destruction, and because of the danger they had brought on the family, he wanted them to be scattered:

> Simeon and Levi are brothers;
> > weapons of violence are their swords.
> May I never come into their council;
> > may I not be joined to their company—
> for in their anger they killed men,
> > and at their whim they hamstrung oxen.
> Cursed be their anger, for it is fierce,
> > and their wrath, for it is cruel!
> I will divide them in Jacob,
> > and scatter them in Israel. (Gen. 49:5–7)

In all this blessing and cursing of his sons, Dinah is never mentioned. Did Jacob even want to see his daughter before he died? If he did, no word from Jacob to her is recorded.

What about Dinah?

The last mention of Dinah is when Jacob dressed down Simeon and Levi for their attack on the unsuspecting city, killing and plundering. Jacob was concerned about the trouble they had brought to him, but the brothers were concerned about honor, saying, "Should our sister be treated like a prostitute?" (Gen. 34:31). That word—*prostitute*—stands as the last description of Dinah. What her brothers wanted to set straight—their sister was not to be treated as if she were some kind of harlot—was unsuccessful. The word *prostitute* and all of its associations with loose morals and slatternly behavior has apparently influenced how many through the years have heard this story and formed their judgment of her. Dinah did not sell her body for sex, but she has been cruelly misjudged over the years. The text does not allow us to hear her cries of despair and anguish and therefore allows some to assume that this silence entails complicity and guilt. It is a very short step from treating her like a prostitute to accusing her of acting like one.

Interpreters often have blamed Dinah for the violence that was done to her. They have seized on the phrase "she went out" and concluded that it was all her fault. Some ancient rabbis ingeniously connected Dinah's "going out" with her mother's "going out" to meet Jacob. When Leah went out to Jacob, she informed him, "You must come in to me; for I have hired you with my son's mandrakes" (Gen. 30:16); and he did what she said and lay with her that night. The rabbinic interpreters argued that she was called "Leah's daughter" because she is just like her mother (*Genesis Rabba* 80 on 30:16). They assumed that Leah acted lewdly when she went out to her husband and then assumed that Dinah also was up to no good when "she went out." Like mother, like daughter (see Ezek. 16:43b–44).

For centuries, this text was also read in the church as a moral tale about the dangers of women leaving the protective confines of their home. The church fathers used this story to warn women to avoid the dangers of the public sphere. Dinah was regarded as a careless nymph who put herself in harm's way, and modest women do not leave the safety of the domicile. If they allow themselves to be seen, they open themselves up for males to desire them—and who knows what will happen next? Simply by going out, it is assumed,

Dinah brought about her own undoing, and a whole city was slaughtered because of her indiscretion. Blame and shame are heaped on her.

We never hear from Dinah, however. She was mute throughout the whole story, a story told only from the males' perspectives. She was acted upon, and we do not know her thoughts or feelings. We do not hear her cry out during her rape; we do not hear her cry out during her confinement; and we do not hear her cry out after she was released and witnessed the strewn corpses in the city. We can only imagine her deep anguish and feelings of complete desolation and powerlessness. She would be forced for the rest of her life to repress her femininity as part of the punishment for supposedly allowing the violation. But her side of the story and her needs were totally ignored and remain untold. The narrator was primarily interested in this story because this attack on Dinah's personal integrity was also an attack on the integrity of the people of the covenant, which needed to be preserved if they were to survive as that people.

Rape, Torture, and Death (Judges 19:1–30)

In Dinah's story, men had all the power; and those with the power were able not only to shape events but also to shape the stories of those events. An even more horrible tale appears in Judges 19, where a woman is brutalized, but it is told as a story of the terrible inhospitality of the men of Gibeah. The woman victim remains mute; we do not even hear her screams.

The story begins when a traveler, a Levite, with his concubine pulled into the town of Gibeah looking for a place to bed down for the night. An old man took him in. To say that the other residents in town were less than hospitable would be an understatement. Some of the local hell-raisers came to the old man's home wanting to drag the visitor out to rape him. The old householder fended off his fellow townsmen by offering them sacrificial lambs, as it were. He placed at their disposal his virgin daughter and the visitor's concubine, and said to them, "Ravish them and do whatever you want to them; but against this man do not do such a vile thing" (Judg. 19:24). The host apparently had a different definition of *vile* than we might have. Raping his guest was vile, but was having their way with his guest's concubine and his own daughter something less than vile? It reveals the premium placed on hospitality to guests and exposes the extreme depravity of the townsmen. To save his own skin, the Levite shoved his concubine out the door and then slammed it tight, as if he were tossing a bone to a pack of wolves.

The rowdy brutes seized and raped the concubine and abused her throughout the night. When they were finally through with her, she crawled back to the house and fell down outside the door, where she lay bruised and broken until daybreak, clinging to the doorsill and barely clinging to life. Her master (the story also calls him "husband") found her there the next morning and icily ordered her, "Get up; let's go" (Judg. 19:28, NIV). She did not answer, so he threw her on his donkey and proceeded on his journey. When he arrived home, he cut her lifeless body into twelve pieces and sent them to the twelve tribes of Israel to announce to them the outrage committed by the men of Gibeah. Israel then commenced a war against the members of that town in revenge for how *this man* was treated. As was the case with Shechem, the vengeance wrought against the guilty parties was overkill. Tens of thousands were annihilated, and their city and surrounding villages were sacked. God appears nowhere in this story.

The Bible makes no comment about the man cutting his concubine into pieces and mailing the parts across the country. The story is about power and politics, about the relationships among the tribes of Israel, and about the betrayal of the political brotherhood among these tribes, which was manifest in the townsmen's desire to abuse this man and their foul treatment of his concubine. No one spoke in behalf of the woman so horribly mistreated. She was a hapless shorn lamb offered up as a sacrifice to save her master, violently gang-raped by thugs, left outside all night in a puddle of her blood, and finally cut up like a side of beef and her body parts shipped around the land. She had no justice, no protection, and no comfort.

What Can We Do for Rape Victims?

These biblical rape victims have no voice or justice—only vengeance designed to restore the reputation of the family. The concubine died from the assault against her; Dinah survived, but one wonders whether life was any better for her after she was rescued and came home. How did her brothers treat her when they stole her from Shechem's household? What did her father say to her when the boys brought her back? Somehow, it does not seem likely that she was greeted with an outpouring of concern for the trauma she had experienced. Her father seized her rape and captivity as an opportunity to wheel and deal for the sake of the family business. The sons sought to avenge their honor and may have felt some satisfaction from the retribution they exacted. Dinah, however, had to live with her own feelings of blame. She lived not only with whatever blame she felt for what had happened to her, but with all the death and destruction that her brothers had visited on innocents to avenge her. Did she want that? She also must have felt shame. Self-blame occurs when we feel responsible for what we have or have not done. Shame emerges from our response to the judgment of others that we are guilty or responsible for what has happened.

She was now regarded as damaged goods, shut up at home with her crazy family for the rest of her life. The Bible never mentions that Dinah marries. Many rabbis, in retelling the story, have tried to make things come out better for Dinah by giving her a child or a husband. In one account, her sexual encounter with Shechem is said to have produced a daughter named Asenath, who became the wife of Joseph in Egypt (*Genesis Rabba* 57:4; 80:11). How this happened, they do not venture to say. Others say that she married Job—not much improvement of her lot there (*Genesis Rabba* 80:4). Others say that she married Simeon (*Genesis Rabba* 80:11). These legends try to turn this rape into something positive, but it may not have turned out well for her. Often, it does not for victims. The memories linger with them for the rest of their lives. It can affect their feelings about God. What kind of God would let this happen? Does God really love and cherish me as the Christians proclaim? How and why could this God ever love and forgive my abuser?

Did anyone care for Dinah? Did anyone help her work through what had happened to her? It does not seem so, but Dinah is still among us, in our congregations and maybe in our own families. What can we do for the victims of violence in our midst?

Victims of violence first experience fear and shock. The fear is usually very realistic. Dinah was helpless. Her fate was in the hands of men who would not even consult her. Would she be married off to this violent man or brought home to live with accusation and shame in her own family? Today's victims live with similar fears. If the perpetrator is a stranger, the victim wonders whether he is still out there, poised to strike again. Are other men like that? she wonders. A sense of basic trust in the world and in oneself is shattered. If the violence was at the hands of an acquaintance or family member, the fear can run even deeper. The victim wonders how she could have so badly misjudged this other person; her whole world tilts. "How could I have been so stupid?" Her ability to make decisions, to trust her own judgment, and to depend on others is shaken or destroyed. Her self-esteem plummets. She may be overcome with shame and self-loathing. Maybe something about her caused this violence. Maybe she deserved it because of something she has done, or just because of who she is.

If she trusts someone enough to share her story, the language that is used is critical. Dinah needed to hear the words *rape* and *violence*. She did not need anyone to suggest that it was some kind of affair or, worse, to be treated "like a prostitute." The Bible is clear that Shechem took her, seized her, and defiled her. She was not asking for it. She was looking for some female companionship and became a victim. Using language to describe what happened that implies that she was guilty and responsible only creates shame and plunges her into reliving the trauma. Not every woman who is raped physically resists her attacker, particularly if she knows him. A woman may have been so well taught not to attack another physically that she is incapable of resisting. She may have been raised to be polite; and, oddly, if the attacker is someone she knows and who couches the rape as seduction, she may not know how to say "Stop!" much less physically resist. A wife whose husband forces her to have sex or to have sex in ways that are hurtful to her may be traumatized and yet not see his behavior for what it is—rape.

Dinah needed to be comforted by having others affirm to her that she did not cause the violence. If she was responsible in some way for leaving herself open to attack—by being naive enough to be in the wrong place at the wrong time, by trusting someone she should not have trusted, by being attracted to someone who was abusive—that does not make her responsible for the attack itself. She needed to hear this over and over from those she trusted with her story, until she believed it herself, and believed that they believed it too. With community support and God's help, she could move from victim to survivor.

Dinah needed to be rescued and made to feel physically and emotionally safe. Instead, she was left for several days captive in the hands of her abuser. Women who have been raped by strangers often need others to help them if they are ever to feel safe again. Such a woman may be afraid to be left alone. A friend can stay with her. Home locks can be changed. Legal charges must be brought so that her abuser can be apprehended and so that she and others are protected from further assault, even if it was a "friend" who violated her. Telling her story to strangers at a police station who ask pointed and potentially humiliating questions may be necessary and traumatizing, and yet it marks the beginning of healing as she takes action to stop the violence he might wreak on others.

If the rape took place in the family, charges also need to be brought and legal resources sought to protect her and other family members from any further harm. It is tragic that many congregations encourage spouses to stay with violent partners, in a misguided understanding of the sanctity of marriage. In the 1980s, a survey of thirty-four denominations disclosed that most pastors were more willing to accept marriage in which some violence was present, even though it is "not God's perfect will," than to advise a separation that would end in divorce. One-third thought women should stay in the home until the abuse became "severe," and nearly half expressed concern that the husband's violence not be overemphasized or used as a "justification" for breaking the marriage commitment. "Pastors who, in order to maintain a marriage, minimize the violence a victim reports to them and disregard her immediate need for safety have mistaken the purpose and substance of marriage in much the same way that the Pharisees mistook the intent of the Sabbath (Mark 2:27)" (Alsdurf and Alsdurf 1988, 169). A wife who has suffered violence and flees is not breaking the marital covenant; it was already broken by the violence. Moreover, the most loving response she can make to this violent man is to stop him from continuing to sin against her. Women who feel the support of their community of faith can begin to take the actions they need to protect themselves and to seek help in holding the violent ones accountable for their actions.

Safety and compassionate listening that helps her recognize herself as victim, not cause, of the violence are major steps. Dinah received neither and was treated like a prostitute, left in her shame and voicelessness. For those women who do achieve a feeling of safety and blame-free acceptance, the next step in healing is often anger. Righteous anger is a necessary part of working through and healing from trauma (K. A. Flynn 2003). A victim is naturally angry with herself and with the perpetrator. But she may also become angry with others who care about her and are also very upset by what has happened, particularly if they try to do some Monday morning quarterbacking, looking for ways that she could have or should have handled herself or her situation differently. If someone had said to Dinah, "What were you thinking, going to town alone?" it would only have poured salt on an already raw wound. She may have asked herself this question over and over, and her shame would have been compounded. But at this stage in healing, she might lash out in anger at this question, responding, "Are you saying this was my fault?"

Expressing anger over such treatment by all the men in her life not only is normal, it is not something that will simply pass and be left behind. A sudden memory or a situation of helplessness can resurrect all of it. "The scar tissue of our wounds is easily broken and the infection of anger is recurrent, like yeast or prostatic infections. One does not cure anger, not even through steady witness and moments of grace" (Brock et al. 2002, 80). The anger therefore needs to be a focus of ongoing prayer for her and for those who care for her.

The metaphor of sailing is most apropos. One simply cannot sail into the wind; the sails cease to function when one turns a sailboat windward. To sail into the wind, one must tack, go first in one direction and then in the other. And so it is with life. To heal, one must tack into anger and then tack into love. To be restored to life, one must "zig" into anger then "zag" into social action. To be renewed, one must think and pray rage, and then one must think and pray love (Brock et al. 2002, 80).

Victims of sexual violence may become angry at God, who, they may imagine, "let" this happen to them. It may be very difficult for them to forgive God, both for the violence and for the lack of justice that they may experience with those who should be concerned about justice. Reading the lament psalms that cry out angrily to God may be therapeutic. They give the sufferer permission to be angry and to voice her anger in no uncertain terms. But sometimes those around the victim may wish instead that she had chosen silence, that she had kept the whole matter secret rather than disrupting everyone's life with the messy truth that does not clean up easily.

The movie *Prince of Tides* is the story of the Wingo family in Charleston, South Carolina, growing up on a tidal island with the burden of shameful family secrets that come close to destroying them all. The father is a brutal, bullying shrimp fisherman, the mother a manipulative, social-climbing beauty. She finally divorces her husband and ascends into the upper class by marrying the banker who had earlier bullied her son, Tom. When Tom's twin sister, Savannah, attempts to commit suicide, Tom is called to New York. Dr. Susan Lowenstein, the psychiatrist working with Savannah, wants help in uncovering the family secrets that her suicidal patient has buried like "a splinter inside her, that she has neglected," to use the words of the doctor, played by Barbra Streisand.

Shameful secrets fester inside Savannah until she is helped to confront them. The most suppressed secret of all relates to "Callenwolde," the woods from which a rapist had stalked their mother and later returned with two escaped convicts on a rainy night years earlier. They attacked the Wingo family while their father was off fishing, raping Tom, Savannah, and their mother, Lila. The rapists are killed after being surprised by the return of their courageous elder brother, Luke Wingo. But Lila pledges her children to absolute secrecy as the bodies are buried on their remote island, lest the news about their shameful humiliation erode the reputation of an already trashy family. It is only after this secret is unearthed and painfully confronted in the course of the story that healing becomes possible. Remaining silent heightened the shame, and a secret on this scale was too much to bear. There are three kinds of family secrets: the ones families hide from the world, the ones they hide from each other, and the ones they hide even from themselves (Pipher 2003).

As painful as it is, talking it through and constructing the story of what happened and how it happened is necessary for victims to rebuild their shattered lives and to become survivors. In studying groups of Christian women who study the Bible and provide support for one another in the crises of life, Susan Rose uses Nelle Morton's wonderful phrase; the women were "hearing one another into speech." Healing comes through sharing our stories with one another in safe and compassionate relationships (Rose 2002). It is not easy to listen to a story of rape, especially when it happened to someone we love. We may want to shut our ears and make it go away and pretend it did not happen. We may want to lash out in anger at the person responsible, except that person is usually not present, and the victim herself gets stung by the backlash. We may want to blame her for letting it happen, even for telling about it and destroying our illusions that all is right with the world and making us have to cope with a crisis we do not want to face.

Moreover, the victim's story takes shape only haltingly, over time; it does not come forth in rational, eloquent prose in the first telling. Victims often tell their stories in a highly emotional, contradictory, and fragmented way, which may undermine others' ability to understand and believe them (Rose 2002). Listening is hard and emotional, too. It takes great patience, compassion, and self-discipline. Because we care, we have to guard against impatience or anger at the one who is trying to share a story that is so painful for both teller and listener. Storytelling that becomes instead an experience of blame and anger at the victim results in hurt and further shattering rather than healing.

Telling her story and being heard begins the process of transformation from victim to survivor. If Dinah had experienced support and been able to tell her story in the biblical narrative, the perpetrator rather than the victim would have been held accountable; telling the story would have exposed the illegitimate use of force, power, and authority. In so doing, the power would have been shifted. To have a voice, to be able to tell one's story and be believed, is power. This empowerment cannot take place in isolation; it can happen only in a community, where people are present, listening and affirming the truth telling.

Beyond the physical harm done by violence and rape, the victim has also experienced denial of her personhood and the presence of God in her at a most basic level. When the trauma goes unspoken and unhealed, she must somehow try to numb the pain. Unfortunately, that numbing also blunts "the power of the spirit to bring life in the aftermath of violence. . . . Nothing erases violence, but, sometimes, the power of presence gets us through" (Brock et al. 2002, 73).

Survivors will always have scars, and sometimes they may wonder, "Will my wounds ever heal?" They never can go back to the way they were before the traumatic experience. On the other hand, by the grace of God, traumas do not have to sink us or define us. Miller notes that *victim* describes a specific moment in time, not permanent self-definition (Miller 2003). The violence becomes her story, but it is only one part of her story. Unfortunately, Dinah appears never to have had the family and community that could help her to find her voice, tell her story, and define her experience rather than being defined by it. She is left voiceless, the rape victim. Retelling her story today rectifies that and may give other victims a voice.

A Community for Survivors

Not all of us have experienced rape or had a family member who was raped or otherwise victimized. But all of us have been through experiences that scar us and bury us in shame. The desire to keep things secret often makes the secret become like Savannah's, a buried splinter that festers. Families and faith communities need to be safe places where we can share our battles in safety and compassion. Too often, the church is the last place people risk sharing their hurts or letting others know the battles they fight. They will ask for prayer and support during times of illness, childbirth, and death, but not in times of family conflict, violence within and outside the family, and heartache. If we would recognize that everyone we meet is in some great life struggle, we would be a lot more kind to them.

Churches and families become faith communities when we can tell our stories to one another and connect our stories to the great themes of God's story, and therein find grace and healing. In an interview in *Biblical Archaeology Review*, Phyllis Trible tells about giving a lecture on the horrific story of the gang-raped, murdered, and dismembered woman in Judges 19. She related:

> After my lecture, a woman came up to me weeping. She said to me, "I didn't know the Bible had a story like that." I expected her to recoil in horror. But she did quite the opposite. She said, "Physically I have not been dismembered, but I have been raped, and I have been psychologically murdered. To know that the Bible is telling my story makes all the difference to me." (Shanks 2006, 52)

It is amazing to think that this story could be a blessing to anybody, but it was a blessing to this woman because it mirrored what she had experienced, and it was in the Holy Bible. Perhaps she thought, if it is in the Bible, God must know and understand what this experience must be like. If this story is read in church, maybe other people can understand it too, or at least they can hear how painful it is and have some inkling of how much love and grace are needed to help heal the wounds.

It is in the telling of our stories that the wounded find healing and that we encourage others to know that their own voice can be heard, too. Dinah's story can be told at last. Moreover, her brothers can find ways to handle their outrage in ways that are compassionate and constructive rather than violent and destructive. Jacob can find ways to reach out to his wounded daughter and embrace her in compassion.

4

Tamar's Story

Commitment to Family against All Odds

Genesis 37–38

Someone once claimed that nothing good in the world has ever been done by well-rounded people. The people who do good work have jagged, broken edges; their edges cut things, shaping their world into new images. This truth applies to most of the folk we meet in Genesis and is certainly true of Judah, the fourth son of Jacob. When we reach the story of Judah and Tamar in the ongoing history of God's covenant family in Genesis, the promise God made to Abraham and Sarah seems on the verge of being dashed by the folly of those who continued his line. Judah, son of Jacob, grandson of Isaac, and great-grandson of Abraham, had pulled up his tent stakes and gone to live among the Canaanites.

The Canaanites were the folks who already occupied the land when Abraham and Sarah first arrived. The Old Testament is strongly biased against them, because they worshiped false gods, notably Baal and Dagon and the goddesses of war and sex, Asherah and Astarte. They tended to be city dwellers who exploited the peasants working the land. Moreover, they engaged in human sacrifice. Their religious practices appealed to the bestial and carnal elements of human nature. Abraham made clear that Canaanites were to be avoided at all costs. When he was old, he had finally been blessed in every way, including the birth of his son Isaac to Sarah. He made the servant in charge of his household swear by the Lord, the God of heaven, and the God of the earth, that he would not get a wife for his son Isaac from the daughters of the Canaanites, who surrounded them (Gen. 24:1–3, 37). He was worried that if Isaac married a Canaanite girl, his heirs would get too chummy with their idolatrous neighbors and be swept away by the tide of Canaanite culture. They would no longer be a people set apart and would lose their distinctive witness to the one God. They would "go native," as it were, lured by all this culture's enticements. Judah's decision to settle in Canaan fulfilled his great-grandfather Abraham's greatest fear. He took up with one of the local women, and the family began to act more and more like their idol-worshiping nemeses.

Sibling Rivalry Run Amok (Genesis 37)

Judah had his reasons for putting distance between himself and the rest of the family. Before we explore the story of his sons and daughter-in-law Tamar, we need to look back at the family in which he had grown up, which was hardly idyllic. His father, Jacob, was a lousy father, as we already witnessed in how he mishandled the rape of his daughter Dinah. Wheeling and dealing his way through life, he seems to have paid little attention to the needs and feelings of those around him, including and especially his children. And there were plenty of children—twelve sons, and we do not know how many daughters. The two matriarchs of the household, Leah and Rachel, had been distracted by their own contest to see who could produce the most sons. The children of Leah may have felt their mother's repudiation as a personal humiliation. All in all, it was a household marked by power struggles, jealousy, and selfish disregard for others.

With these dynamics as a backdrop, Jacob made it worse by playing favorites among his children, singling out the two sons of his beloved wife Rachel for special attention over the sons of Leah and the concubines. Jacob made it clear that he loved Joseph, the firstborn of Rachel, more than any of his other sons. He decked him out in a richly adorned robe, an insensitive gesture that only deepened his other sons' aggravation with their already uppity brother (Gen. 37:3–4). Joseph foolishly flaunted his status as the favorite child, tattled on his older brothers to Dad (Gen. 37:2), and bragged about his grandiose dreams in which he would lord it over all of them. He fanned the embers of sibling rivalry into flames of murderous hatred (Gen. 37:5–8). The ten older brothers wickedly plotted to do away with the dream weaver by throwing him into a pit for the wild animals to devour. These brothers were not children; Joseph himself was seventeen at the time (Gen. 37:2). Their actions were not the pranks of older brothers turning out the lights and making spooky sounds when their younger brother is down in the eerie, dank basement bringing up some firewood. They were not trying to scare the bejabbers out of him; very simply, they were grown men plotting to kill a younger brother. Jacob may have been a terrible father, their mother's mistreatment a sore spot, and Joseph a pain in the neck, but that does not excuse attempted murder.

Judah, brother number four, was in the thick of the conspiracy but saved Joseph's life by coming up with the scheme to make some profit by selling Joseph to passing traders (Gen. 37:26–27). Judah's suggestion to sell Joseph as a slave to Midianite traveling merchants won the day and foiled the plan of Reuben, the eldest. Reuben had thought that once the brothers had gone, he would sneak back, rescue his brother and increase his standing with his father. It is not clear whether Judah's plan was simply an attempt to make money or in fact was a cowardly way to save his brother from his siblings' lust for blood. But if he truly was concerned about Joseph's fate, there is no evidence of it. He certainly did not go running after the traders, seeking to buy back his brother.

Violence done by strangers is frightening. But violence done by family is doubly horrifying. We expect older brothers to look out for and defend younger siblings, not to kill them or sell them into slavery. Perhaps violence between siblings is the most neglected form of violence in our own society. We have heard stories of siblings being beaten, tied up, and locked in closets, and of limbs broken in tussles with one another while adults were absent or unaware. On a more minor level, siblings punch one another and strike out at one another, and too often the response of adults is to let them "work it out among themselves," saying, "What's a little roughhousing going to hurt? Boys will be boys." Story after story in the Bible shows that God's children do not work things out on their own. They hurt and even kill one another. These boys carried their petty childhood squabbles and jealousies into adulthood.

Joseph was brought down to Egypt and brought down in more ways than one—from well-dressed, most-favored son to a slave sold to the highest bidder. The tattered family fabric began to show worse signs of being ripped apart and, along with it, God's promise to Abraham. "At that time," the narrator tells us, Judah left his brothers and moved away (Gen. 38:1). Evidently, he could not bear to live in the face of his father's grief any more than he was able to bear Joseph's gloating about his favored status. He left home, seeking to run away from his guilt and to leave family behind. Physical relocation can give us a sense of fresh air and a new beginning, but it does not free us of family entanglements, no matter how far we run or how seldom we call home. He carried the family baggage strapped to his back—the guilt for his brother's enslavement, the conspiracy to deceive his father about his death, and his father's inconsolable grief. It must have weighed him down and haunted him. No wonder the family he established in his new home faced troubles of its own.

Judah and His Canaanite Family (Genesis 38:1–10)

Judah settled in Canaan and married a Canaanite, Shua, who bore him three sons, Er, Onan, and Shelah. He apparently found Canaanite women to his liking and married off his eldest son, Er, to a local woman named Tamar. Er died, it says, because he was evil, but the text is silent about what he did to warrant divine capital punishment. It does not seem to matter to the narrator; Judah must have grieved the loss of his firstborn, but, again, the text is silent about it. The silence makes Judah seem callous compared to his father, Jacob, who grieved so desperately over the loss of Joseph. The narrator may have wanted to make a deliberate contrast between the two fathers. Now Judah, the brother who conspired to kill his father's son, knew what it was like to lose a son.

Tamar's first marriage was to a man so evil that God struck him dead. It may have been a relief to her, but his death left her in a delicate situation. A woman who came from outside a clan had problems being integrated into the clan in the best of circumstances—and Tamar was a Canaanite in the home of Israelites. Bearing her husband's children was the only way for her to become cemented into the family. The children become a visible token that she fully belonged. If she had no children, she never completely became a member of the family. Er was cut down in the prime of his life, leaving Tamar childless and therefore family-less.

Her uncertain status was compounded by the fact that a woman did not inherit her husband's estate. If a woman's husband died, the inheritance passed on to the children. A widow's economic life depended on having children who could support and defend her. Without children, she could either hope that she would be treated as a charity case by her husband's clan or go back home to her father's house and hope to be taken in there. A childless widow fit securely nowhere and was vulnerable to exploitation. Her father-in-law could force her to marry again. But because she was no longer a virgin, her bride value to another suitor was decreased dramatically.

The other option to resolve her plight was the custom of the levirate marriage, an ancient form of security net for the childless young widow. It rescued her from limbo and gave her some measure of protection. Our culture is familiar with surrogate mothers and fathers who provide the means for infertile couples to have their own children. Levirate marriage was somewhat comparable, except it had more far-reaching social dimensions. *Levir* is Latin, for "husband's brother." The husband's brother was supposed to have intercourse with his widow to provide her with (male) offspring. The brother became the surrogate father of the son born from the union. The child secured the young widow's place in her husband's family, provided someone who could watch over her in her old age, and honored her dead husband by giving him a measure of immortality by continuing his name. This custom forced both parties to submit—the widow out of necessity, the brother out of duty. It was loveless copulation for the purpose of producing children. Tamar intended to remain faithful to her dead husband, Er, by providing offspring for his name, even though the narrator tells us that he had been a wicked man.

Er's brother Onan was the second-oldest brother and so the one to take on this responsibility to carry on his brother's name. He was ordered by his father to do his duty by her and to raise up offspring for his brother (Gen. 38:8). When the specifics of the levirate law are spelled out in Deuteronomy 25:5–9, it declares that if the brother refuses to honor this responsibility to his late brother, he must endure public humiliation and be proclaimed a louse who had forsaken his duty. The rejected widow could, with impunity, yank off his sandal and then spit in his face. If such was the custom in the time of Judah, Onan did not want to endure such a public humiliation. When his father ordered him to lie with Tamar, therefore, he appeared to comply with the custom. He was no less wicked than his brother Er was said to have been, however, and resorted to sneaky sexual sabotage to shirk his responsibility. He used coitus interruptus as a form of birth control, preventing Tamar from conceiving. He used her sexually—how many times the text does not say—and basically treated her like a cheap prostitute. He cheated his brother from having descendants and Tamar from her place in the family.

Onan's consent to have intercourse with Tamar but maneuvering to avoid actually impregnating her made sense from an economic point of view. With Er's death, Onan had moved into the position of firstborn, but providing an heir for Er would drastically reduce the size of the inheritance he was now in position to receive. The firstborn received a double portion of the inheritance. He may have thought, "If she has a child by me, my own family will get the short end of the stick when it comes to our father's inheritance. It will go to her kids bearing my brother's name, not mine!" Onan continued the self-centered tendencies that marked this family with cheating and deception, repeating with a somewhat different twist the path of his grandfather Jacob, who also coveted his brother's inheritance and used duplicity to get it. The family kettle of strife kept boiling. Moreover, he could enjoy a sexual relationship with Tamar without taking on any responsibility. Was Tamar aware of Onan's strategy for avoiding impregnating her? We do not know. She is silent and evidently powerless.

God was not powerless, however. God struck down Onan for his wickedness, like his brother Er before him (and, we might add, like the flood generation and the cities of Sodom and Gomorrah). This element in the story may be no less troubling to us than the unseemly events that follow. Why were these two men struck down and not all the other wicked men we have encountered in these stories? It seems that God appears to be arbitrary and violent, but the deaths of Er and Onan are a necessary element in God's plan. The writer was not trying to convey something about the nature of God, but rather, something about the inevitable consequences of sin. It brings death in its wake. Sometimes that death comes immediately; sometimes it becomes woven into the fabric of life itself. Death is the literal result for Onan, but also death to Tamar's hope to have a child and to secure a home for herself in her husband's family.

A Daughter-in-Law Ignored (Genesis 38:11)

A distant hope still remained, however. There was Shelah, the youngest brother, but he was much too young, and Tamar had to wait for him to come of age to perform this duty. Judah put her off: "Just wait until the lad is old enough."

Judah dealt with Tamar just as dishonorably as did his son Onan. She was under his authority, since marriage for women in that day meant being passed from the control of their fathers and brothers to that of their husbands and fathers-in-law. She was also supposed to be under his protection, but he offered her nothing. He had lost two sons; perhaps he viewed her as cursed and bringing a curse on everyone who came into intimate contact with her. He did not want to tempt fate three times, so he sent her back to her father's house with the promise that when Shelah was a little older, she would be given to him. Judah told her to sit as a widow in her father's house until that time. In other words, "Don't call me, I'll call you." He may also have been thinking, "Let her father bear the expense of her upkeep." Putting Tamar off like this denied her status, disregarded her well-being, and basically negated her personhood. It would become clear as the years passed that Judah had no intention of following through on his obligation to her. He wanted to get rid of her and was making empty promises to do just that. In essence, Judah consigned Tamar to oblivion. If he had released her, she might have married again. With no financial security and no freedom to marry anyone else, she became an outcast both from Judah's home and in her father's house.

Judah appears to be cold and heartless. If he could sell his own brother into slavery, it was nothing to turn his daughter-in-law out into the cold. It was no wonder that he had raised two wicked sons, and there was not much hope that Shelah would turn out any different.

Tamar was left for "a long time" in limbo (Gen. 38:12). She waited in her father's house, continuing to wear her widow's clothes, signifying that she actually belonged to the house of Judah. Why she wanted to stay attached to Judah's house with all its faults and after her maltreatment may seem a mystery. Unfortunately, she had no other choices that were any better.

Covering Tamar's Eyes and Opening Judah's (Genesis 38:12–23)

The years went by. Shelah grew up, and Judah never called Tamar. Death continued to visit the house of Judah; his wife Shua, mother of the three sons, died, and Judah grieved—and recovered from his grief.

Up to this point in the story, Tamar has been the object of the verbs as she was acted upon by others: she was taken as a wife, Onan was told to go in to her, she was told to remain a widow and to go to her father's house. When she is the subject of the verbs, she is at first a model of compliance: she went as instructed to her father's house. She knew that Shelah had grown up. How many years had passed? Yet nary a peep from Judah. Her quiet patience and obedience shifted into decisive and cunning action.

When she was told that her father-in-law was going to Timnah to shear sheep (the equivalent of the National Sheep-shearers' Convention), she sprang into action, taking matters into her own hands. She slipped off her mourning garments, which she had been wearing all these years, decked herself out in more appealing garb, and disguised herself with a veil. A woman behind a veil is seductive, according to Song of Solomon 4:1, 3; 6:7. Tamar took up a position by the roadside on the way to Timnah where Judah would have to pass by.

The place where she waited is identified as "the entrance to Enaim." There is an ironic play on words in the Hebrew, since the name is related to the Hebrew word for "eyes." Tamar covers her eyes with a veil to deceive Judah. When he came to the place where Tamar sat, however, he was blinded by his lust and saw what he thought was only a hooker willing to sell her body to him, not his daughter-in-law. His eyes would be opened much later, when it was too late, but his eyes would be opened to his duty in new ways, and he would also view Tamar in an entirely new light.

This story harks back to Jacob, who awoke in the morning to find he had just slept with Leah, not Rachel. Judah's blindness is not so surprising, however. He had never really seen Tamar as a person with needs and for whom he was responsible. He had made an early attempt to care for her by ordering Onan to lie with her. But evidently he never asked why no pregnancy ensued. He went through the motions, just as Onan had done. He had gone through the motions with his little brother, too, managing to spare him from death, only to allow him to be sold into slavery and never attempting to rescue him. Judah talked about responsibility, but when something depended on him, he was not there. He had never connected with Tamar, treating her as a nonperson. It had been years since he sent her away. It is ironic that only now, when she was wearing a veil, that he finally "saw" Tamar. As a sexual object—not a person—she attracted his notice.

Some claim, "The Lord helps those who help themselves," but Tamar's attempt to help herself by stooping to prostitution seems a bit over the top. It may not have violated Canaanite custom to try to have a child by her father-in-law, but such a relationship would be explicitly condemned later in the Jewish law. Technically, this was incest: "You shall not uncover the nakedness of your daughter-in-law: she is your son's wife; you shall not uncover her nakedness" (Lev. 18:15). This prohibition occurs in a long list of sexual taboos, and the law goes on to explain that the perversions in the list are the practices of the nations whom God is casting out because of their defilement (Lev. 18:24). God commands:

> But you shall keep my statutes and my ordinances and commit none of these abominations, either the citizen or the alien who resides among you (for the inhabitants of the land, who were before you, committed all of these abominations, and the land became defiled); otherwise the land will vomit you out for defiling it, as it vomited out the nation that was before you. For whoever commits any of these abominations shall be cut off from their people. So keep my charge not to commit any of these abominations that were done before you, and not to defile yourselves by them: I am the LORD your God. (Lev. 18:26–30)

What Tamar did was not supposed to work. It is classified as an abomination. Carol Smith observes: "When women are in trouble in Genesis, the solution is often provided by a divine figure—so, the 'barren women' stories are constructed so that the threat to the family line is overcome through divine intervention, and Hagar is supported in her time of banishment by an angel of God" (Smith 1992, 24). The problem here, however, was not that Tamar was barren. It did not require divine intervention to open a womb; it required the transformation of Judah to open his heart.

Though Tamar did not know it, what was at stake was not simply her inclusion in the Judah clan. This strange story is part of a larger story of a family line that was in danger of dying out. "If the line had died out, the subsequent history of the nation, and hence of the world, would have been different." Judah's irresponsibility was threatening the family's future (Smith 1992, 22). What was at stake was the continuation of the covenant family under Judah's leadership, who had, up to now, abdicated that responsibility. What was at stake was the continuation of the people of the promise that will lead to King David, the lion of the tribe of Judah, and culminate in the coming of the Son of David, the Son of God.

We witness Tamar's sheer tenacity in the midst of great duress. She took an incredible risk. It was the kind of courageous risk taking that has marked this covenant family. In a strange way, after a fruitless, passive wait of many years, she stepped out on faith. She did not try to seduce Judah. If he saw her by the side of the road and passed on by, there was nothing that she could do. If he recognized her during intercourse, he certainly would have exposed her and had her stoned. If she did not become pregnant from this encounter, all of her efforts would have been for naught. So many ifs, but she would not be denied. Somehow she knew that he would stop and go in to her. She knew that if she turned up pregnant, her irate father-in-law would do something like try to burn her at the stake. So she was prepared for the worst. She was not only courageous, she was also deceptive.

Risk taking and deception were at the core of Jacob's family. They engaged in one deception after another. Judah deceived her by sending her home to her father to wait for a call that would never come. She now deceived him with her garment—reminiscent of the way that Judah and his brothers had deceived their father with Joseph's blood-spattered garment as evidence that he had been torn to pieces by animals. The deceit had come full circle.

What ensued is like a comedy of mistaken identity, except that so much was at stake. Tamar must have known Judah's vices; he was so predictable. He was a widower, away from home on a business trip, looking for some entertainment and sexual release from a local lady of pleasure, hopefully in anonymity. He would probably say, if cornered, that he was only looking for some way to relieve his loneliness and to forget his sorrows. He spied Tamar sitting by the roadway, apparently open for business and free for the moment. His brother Joseph would resist the seductions of Potiphar's wife in the next chapter of Genesis, but Judah was different. His desire was aroused, he turned to her, and he asked permission to come in to her tent. The first words Tamar speaks in the whole story are: "What will you give me, that you may come in to me?" (Gen. 38:16). Her silence to this point was a sign of her absolute powerlessness. Until now, her voice had been muted. The only access to power she had was through sex. Judah not only did not recognize her with his eyes, but his ears did not recognize her voice, this woman who had lived in his household for years. Obviously, he had never really seen her or heard her; she was just a piece of furniture, not a family member.

We do not know how she felt about the prospect of sexual liaison with her father-in-law, or what she felt about anything that had happened to her. We can only guess. We can be fairly sure that her action was driven by her anger over the injustice she had suffered at his hands and by desperation—a primal urge to survive and even to vindicate herself. How must she have felt, dressing up like a prostitute and then placing herself in that vulnerable position? How long did she sit there, waiting and mulling her situation over in her mind? How angry must she have been to have to sink to this? What if Judah or his traveling companion recognized her? Judah had the right to have her killed for prostitution. Did other men proposition her before Judah came down the road? She must have carried on an inner conversation with herself, steeling her nerves and steadying her resolve. Hers was a desperate, courageous act. Courage is not a characteristic of fearless people doing brave deeds. Courage is frightened people doing what needs to be done.

When Judah offered to send a kid from his flock, she accepted, but only on the condition that he leave some collateral with her until the goat arrived. She required his cylindrical seal for signatures, which was worn around the neck with a cord, and his staff that would have been personalized with some distinguishing mark. It was like leaving an engraved watch in a brothel—embarrassing for any respectable man if it should ever come to light. He would also be hesitant to try to reclaim his property from such a place, once he was thinking clearly about what he had done. In the heat of the moment, Judah was willing to part with the personally identifying items for the chance to satiate his sexual urge.

After he returned home, Judah sent his friend Hirah, a Canaanite wise to the ways of the world who had been on the business trip with him, on the embarrassing errand to pay his bill for the prostitute. Hirah would know where to find her, or so Judah assumed. It is interesting that Judah wanted to pay his obligation to Tamar the harlot but reneged on his obligation to Tamar the daughter-in-law. But it probably had nothing to do with responsibility; he simply was keen to reclaim his personal identification.

When Hirah referred to her, he used a term other than *harlot*. He identified her as a "shrine prostitute." Perhaps he wanted to raise her status a bit. The two terms may be synonymous, or perhaps Hirah employed a "euphemism—comparable to our substitution of the term 'courtesan' for the cruder expression 'whore'" (Bird 1989, 126). Maybe Hirah could not imagine that his friend would demean himself by having sexual congress with a cheap hussy sitting by the wayside. As a Canaanite, Hirah had no qualms about Judah engaging a shrine prostitute. For an Israelite, however, engaging a shrine prostitute was even more disgraceful than hiring a standard streetwalker. Temple prostitution associated with the Canaanite fertility cult was part of the culture that Abraham had found so abhorrent.

Hirah was unsuccessful in locating the woman who serviced Judah. She was nowhere to be found, and Judah's personal effects and insignia had vanished with her. No one had seen her or knew anything about her. When Hirah reported to Judah that he had been unsuccessful in finding her, Judah responded by telling him to forget about it and to keep things quiet "lest we be laughed at." He was worried about being the brunt of the barbershop gossip. The guys would get quite a laugh out of Judah being duped by a prostitute. Many "johns" have been robbed by prostitutes who take their wallets, knowing that their customers would be too embarrassed to report the theft to the police lest word get out—particularly back home. Judah was in the same boat, it seems. The cheap trollop turned out to be more expensive than he had bargained for. His reputation was more important than getting back his personal items. Chalk it up to experience, he thought, which would make him more wary the next time.

The Showdown (Genesis 38:24–26)

Little did Judah suspect the surprise that was coming. His trip and his choice to satisfy his sexual needs with a harlot corresponded with Tamar's fertile time in the month. The timing was impeccable, and Tamar became pregnant. Word came to him that she was pregnant "as a result of her whoredom" (Gen. 38:24). The story does not say who informed Judah, or how they reached the conclusion that she had been prostituting herself, although there were few other explanations.

Judah had not given her to Shelah, nor had he released her to remarry. The reader knows the full story: she conceived by *his* whoring.

On the basis of these reports, Judah pronounced her guilty and sentenced her to death without even seeing her. His moral outrage reflects the sexual double standard that he took for granted. Men—including Israelites as well as Canaanites—could exercise their sexual freedom and would not be condemned for visiting prostitutes. They might be laughed at if they should get snookered as Judah had been, but there was no punishment—not even a slap on the wrist, much less the death penalty. They reasoned that having sex with a prostitute was not committing adultery, because that did not violate another man's rights. The prostitute did not belong to anyone, according to this reasoning. The woman's sexuality, by contrast, had to be carefully guarded, to ensure that any children she bore were her husband's, so that his line would not be defiled. Ironically, Judah surmised correctly that the child was conceived by whoring, but it was, in effect, her husband's child. The line had not been defiled.

As head of the family, Judah was all-powerful. He wielded the power of life and death over Tamar. Prior to this, he had not treated her as one who belonged to his house. He had done little to ensure that her needs were met, but he was swift to step in when he thought that she threatened the honor of his household. He set himself up as the judge, and he turned out to be a hanging judge. Perhaps he thought to himself that at last he had a way out of the pesky problem of this daughter-in-law. Take her out to be burned at the stake! It was an unusually harsh sentence, pronounced on her when she was not even present to defend herself. He denied her the chance for life by having offspring through Er's brother, but he was quick to offer her death for despoiling the family's honor.

Although she had been living for years in her father's house, her father apparently had no say in her fate. She deserved death for bringing shame to the family of Judah. Even today throughout the world, thousands of women are killed for tarnishing the family honor for some sexual impropriety. Judah's heavy-handed punishment may have been motivated by a desire to get rid of an unpleasant reminder of his failure to fulfill his responsibility. He was the one who acted most shamefully.

When they were dragging Tamar out to burn her, she pulled her trump card from her sleeve, the items that Judah had left in pledge, and sent them to Judah with the message, "Recognize, pray," that is, "Please take notice" (authors' translation). These are the exact same words the brothers used with Jacob to have him identify the coat of his son Joseph (Gen. 37:32). She was probably not so coarse as to say to him, "Remember these little doodads, big boy?" but it had the same effect. He had self-righteously turned a family crisis into a public hanging, and she used the occasion to humiliate him instead. He was an even worse laughingstock than he had feared. According to the law laid down in Leviticus 20:12, "If a man lies with his daughter-in-law, both of them shall be put to death; they have committed perversion; their blood is upon them." If she was to be burned, then Judah should be burned as well. But it was a man's world, and Judah exercised his prerogative to call the whole thing off. As it turned out, "it was only the patriarch's cheeks which burned" (Schepps 1976, 79).

In fact, it was a moment of transformation for Judah. To his considerable credit, Judah finally took responsibility for Tamar and confessed *publicly* that she was righteous, not he. The only shame brought on his house had come through him, not her. He had been a poor brother, father, father-in-law, and representative of the God of the covenant.

A Righteous Commitment to Family

His pronouncement that Tamar was righteous means that we may have to rethink what it means to be righteous. Does it mean that commitment to family is akin to righteousness? Righteous are those determined to preserve family solidarity and well-being? Or does it mean that risk taking can lead to righteousness? Righteous are the audacious risk takers. Or does it mean that those who are faithful to promises and demand faithfulness of others are righteous? Tamar may have been a Canaanite, but she modeled the faithfulness of God who makes and keeps covenants. She believed that Judah would do right by her and faithfully waited—for years. When it became clear that he would not do right by her on his own, she courageously pushed him to act like the responsible family member he had never been. Judah's own family taught him the self-centered power strategies to leverage one's way in a family. Tamar the Canaanite modeled and held him to a higher standard of righteousness.

It marked a new beginning for Judah. The two wicked sons he lost were replaced—from the same woman who would not accept defeat and acted righteously. Out of this seamy and sordid incident, he learned to act righteously. We see the evidence of this transformation in Genesis 44:18–34. The crisis of a famine evidently had brought the family together again. When the brothers trekked to Egypt to buy grain during a period of famine, unbeknownst to them they encountered their long-lost brother Joseph, who was now second-in-command to Pharaoh. Joseph demanded that they bring their youngest brother, Benjamin, on the next trip. To test the heart of Judah, who had clearly become the leader, Joseph framed Benjamin by placing his own silver cup in Benjamin's bag and then feigning anger when the supposed theft was discovered. As a consequence, Benjamin was to be made a slave in Joseph's house as punishment.

Judah stepped up to tell the sad tale of his father's special love for this child of his old age and the last of his mother's children. The other brother, he presumed, was dead and lost forever. His father would die to lose him and acknowledged this by quoting his father's own words, "My wife [Rachel] bore me two sons" (Gen. 44:27), as though Leah's boys—including Judah himself—did not count. Gone was the former jealousy and homicidal enmity over being left out of his father's affections. Judah offered himself in trade as a hostage for his brother's and his father's sake. He would become a slave to Joseph in place of the boy. The formerly calloused, hard-hearted Judah now feared "to see the suffering that would come upon [his] father" (Gen. 44:34). He too now knew what it is like to lose sons. Judah, who had been willing to sell a brother into slavery, offered himself to save a brother from slavery. He modeled what Jesus taught: "You know that among the Gentiles those whom they recognize as their rulers lord it over them, and their great ones are tyrants over them. But it is not so among you; but whoever wishes to become great among you must be your servant, and whoever wishes to be first among you must be slave of all. For the Son of Man came not to be served but to serve, and to give his life a ransom for many." (Mark 10:42–45). And, "No one has greater love than this, to lay down one's life for one's friends" (John 15:13).

For Tamar, the confrontation with Judah was the beginning of her becoming a full member of this wild and woolly clan that God promised would become a blessing to all the nations. Her place was ensured among her husband's people. Family ties were important to her, and she stopped at nothing to secure them. It was not just the pregnancy that earned her a place in this family, however; she risked believing that Judah could act righteously, even though he had failed her time and again. Her righteousness called forth righteousness in him. For the first time, he had overcome the limitations of his own family's deceit and power maneuvering not by running away, but by confronting them in his own life. He saw himself, perhaps for the first time, as a consequence. And also as a consequence, he could finally truly see and care for others. He learned to his surprise and mortification how important family is, and we next see him taking charge of a prickly, quarreling band of brothers and helping to restore unity and make them family again.

Tamar had a special birth, twins no less, both struggling to come out of the womb, reminiscent of the twins Jacob and Esau. Judah lost two boys who were wicked, and by God's grace receives two boys, Zerah and Perez, from an encounter that seems to be utterly wicked. The scarlet thread tied around the hand of the twin whose hand came out first may remind us that they were conceived in the red-light district. But this one would not be the firstborn. The other twin came out first, to the surprise of the midwife, who exclaimed, "What a breach you have made for yourself!" (Gen. 38:29). And he got stuck with the name Perez, that is, "Breach," for the rest of his life. It is an apt name, because this whole story is a breach of expectations as well as cultural taboos. Perez will become the ancestor of Boaz (Ruth 4:12), who through Ruth will father Obed, who fathers Jesse, who fathers King David. Tamar is linked to Ruth in Matthew's genealogy of Jesus. They were both foreigners and both widows, both remained loyal to their husband's families, and both took matters into their own hands to have sons (through levirate traditions) and challenged their husband's family to live righteously. Tamar was the wrong kind of wife because she was a Canaanite, the people whom Abraham warned against, but somehow through her the purposes of God were fulfilled. She brought life by continuing the line of Judah. She brought transformation by reminding Judah of the call to be righteous. The only begotten son of God traced his lineage back to some strangely begotten heirs, and we see the steady, often invisible hand of God guiding things along through what look like impassable roadblocks.

Zerah's line did not fare as well. He fathered Zabdi, who fathered Carmi, who fathered Achan, who provoked the anger of the Lord to burn hot against the Israelites because he tried to squirrel away some devoted things during the invasion of Jericho (Joshua 7). He wound up being stoned and burned and buried under a pile of more stones hurled at his body for his violation. This family is not the holy family and does not escape sin's stranglehold that grips all humans.

If we focus only on Tamar, can we say that it has a happy ending? No marriage follows—it is all a matter of securing one's place in a family. She may not have ever received her heart's desire, but she received what she needed. The story shows once again that God chooses the side of the oppressed (Bos 1992, 122). On the other hand, it is easy to slip into the ancient world's assumption that it took marriage for a woman to find fulfillment: "A woman, without her man, is nothing." If the punctuation is changed only slightly, it makes a radically different statement: "A woman: without her, man is nothing." Surely, Tamar knew that it was her persistence and courage that led to the transformation of Judah and, beyond, to the band of brothers that would become the grand patriarchs of Israel.

5

Michal's Story
With a Family Like This, Who Needs Enemies?

1 Samuel 17–18:20

Michal's story seems to begin as a love story. The narrator lets it be known, "Now Saul's daughter Michal loved David" (1 Sam. 18:20). David cut a dashing figure as a great military hero loved by all in Israel and Judah (1 Sam. 18:16), but his growing popularity threatened King Saul, Michal's father. Saul became insanely jealous (with an emphasis on *insane*) and increasingly paranoid about David. That danger factor may have made David seem all the more exciting and attractive to Michal. The story begins like a fairy tale, with a princess and a handsome warrior, but we know that trouble is brewing in this relationship because he is the rival of her father the king. Instead of an evil stepmother trying to do in the princess, we have a murderous father trying to destroy the would-be prince.

Michal was the youngest of Saul's five children (1 Sam. 14:49). She first appears in the biblical story when David had reached the pinnacle of popularity after slaying the Philistine giant Goliath. Goliath had confounded the Israelite army and threatened to turn the Israelites into slaves (1 Sam. 17:8–9). The young buck David saved the day when he felled Goliath with a single missile from his celebrated slingshot. David's resulting fame and continuing battlefield successes may have agitated King Saul, who was used to getting all of the accolades, but they only fed Michal's attraction to him as the reigning toast of Judah. Earlier, Saul had offered Michal's older sister Merab to David in marriage as a reward for his courage and success on the battlefield, with the ulterior motive of keeping David loyal and under his wing. David had turned down that offer, modestly pointing out that his humble stock as a sheepherder made him unworthy to be grafted into the royal line. His humility was no doubt quite becoming. A determined, moon-eyed Michal decided to risk letting her love for David become known.

The statement that Michal was in love with David (1 Sam. 18:20) is the only one in the Bible that explicitly announces that a woman loves a man. She was evidently a strong woman, willing to go after what she wanted. And she wanted David. She must have convinced herself that though he may not have wanted Merab, he would not be able to resist her, Merab's younger sister. Michal had known David for years. He had been hanging around her family since Saul had brought him home as a young man to be his attendant. Now, at Saul's insistence, David had moved into the royal household permanently. Saul sent David on mission after mission, and every time he came home the victor. With each victory, Michal's love grew. With each cheer for this youthful, handsome, victorious warrior, Saul's resentment grew.

Why Is Daddy So Mad? (1 Samuel 15)

To understand how Saul's green-eyed jealousy turned into red rage, we need to turn back several chapters to trace Saul's own rise to power. In his younger days, Saul had also been a good and humble man, a handsome and noble warrior. He became the first God-anointed king of Israel, and like David, he also had pummeled the enemies of the Israelites in battle. One victory in particular opened the door for his downfall. After defeating the Amalekites, he began to believe that he, not God, knew what was best for his people. He mistook his success in battle as a tribute to his own strength and wisdom rather than God's. His distancing himself from God was a gradual process, so gradual that no one noticed, except God and God's mouthpiece, the prophet Samuel. Saul increasingly ignored God's leading. Before the battle with the Amalekites, through the clear voice of the prophet Samuel, God commanded Saul to destroy everything that belonged to the enemy. But Saul wanted to be popular with his soldiers, and, after their hard-won victory, he let his troops keep the best of the captured livestock rather than wasting it in what seemed like senseless destruction. The army was dreaming of a huge barbeque dedicated to God. Surely God would appreciate the sentiment, Saul thought, and the men deserved a party after such a stellar victory. They would also love him—King Saul—all the more for allowing them to indulge their appetites. Saul was insecure and self-centered; what others thought of him was more important than obeying God. So party they did. God's expectation, as voiced by the prophet Samuel, that a whole people be destroyed, including infants and children, may disturb us. This God, who expects those who worshiped other gods to be annihilated, frightens us. The story, however, does not focus on how God could order such destruction. Its focus is on how Saul was more interested in gaining popularity with his troops than in obeying God.

The prophet Samuel, never one to mince words, had communicated clearly that the royal barbeque was an act of rebellion against God. Since Saul had followed his own counsel rather than God's, Samuel informed him that he would no longer lead Israel. God's Spirit departed from Saul that day (1 Sam. 15:26).

It is easy to turn control of our lives over to God when we do not feel big enough or strong enough or wise enough to face the challenges before us. It is easy to pray for God's guidance and presence when we know we cannot otherwise survive. But when we meet only with success, and others acclaim us as strong, or wise, or great in some way, it is so easy to believe they must be right. Saul fell into this trap and forgot that the victory was God's, not his. He forgot that it was not his own strength but God's leading that was behind his success. He abandoned God's direction and grew increasingly cranky with the prophet Samuel, who kept reminding him of the error of his ways.

Though Saul said he was sorry for his disobedience, he expressed his regret only after Samuel confronted him with his sin and told him that he would lose his throne over what he had done. In fact, instead of admitting that he was wrong and taking personal responsibility for his actions, Saul made matters worse by trying to pin the blame on others. "I have sinned," he said, but he then went on to say, "I was afraid of the men and so I gave in to them. Now I beg you, forgive my sin" (1 Sam. 15:24–25a, authors' paraphrase). It was a shallow repentance. He tried to excuse himself by pointing to the baneful influence of those around him—"It's really their fault!" He did not say, "I am the leader you have appointed over them. I should have done what I knew was right; I could have said no to them. I take full blame." He refused to accept any guilt—it was his men's fault. He just wanted God to forgive and forget and to let things go on as before, with him still wielding the scepter over Israel. True repentance would have required him to take responsibility for what he had done, to change, to put God back in charge of his life.

Though we may not be planning holy barbeques with the spoils of war, Saul's sin, false repentance, and excuse making sound all too familiar. He responded to God's confrontation through Samuel with, "Please don't be mad at me any more," rather than undertaking a critical self-examination and determining, with God's help, to change. If he had his way, God would just forgive him, ignore what he had done, let things go on as they had been going, and all would be well with the world. He would not have to do anything.

False repentance says, "Please don't be mad at me," and tries to duck any responsibility. It says, "You need/ought to forgive me; the relationship is in your hands," without taking responsibility for what we have done. We want to just say to one another and to God, "I'm sorry. Now you have to still love me." True repentance, on the other hand, means saying, "I did this" and "I will try to do differently from now on." True repentance does not chide others for our behavior. Reconciliation with the one we have wronged needs to be based on our accepting responsibility for what we have done and turning in a new direction. It requires us to change. The prophet Ezekiel says that to repent is to get a new mind and a new heart, and that means trying never to repeat the harmful behavior (Ezek. 36:26–27). Quick forgiveness short-circuits this renewal. Samuel offers Saul no such repentance. "Forgive and forget" is cheap, putting all the responsibility on the one wronged. It cannot restore broken relationships, either relationships between us and God or relationships with one another. Would God have restored the covenant with Saul if he had truly repented? Just looking at the story of David reveals that God forgives and restores covenants with those who repent. But Saul refused.

Did Saul's family begin to feel the shame of their father's weakness, because he gave in to his soldiers rather than being a strong spiritual and military leader? Did Michal cringe to see her father's moral frailty? And worse, to hear him whine that others made him do it rather than taking responsibility for his actions?

Saul had turned from God, and so God turned from Saul as the leader of the people. The vacuum of God's absence was filled by an evil spirit that began to torment Saul. His servants, in desperation, suggested musical therapy as a way to calm him. They would find someone to play music for him during his fits of anguish, to quiet his soul. There was no "easy listening" radio station to create a calming atmosphere; they needed a live person with a live instrument. Enter David, the shepherd. David was perhaps still a teenager before his unexpected victory against Goliath. He could play the lyre and was a handsome lad, healthy from chasing sheep over the hillsides. He was very much like Saul as a young man. The similarities may not have been lost on Saul, but he could not have foreseen that this lad, who seemed to him to still be wet behind the ears, would become his bitterest rival to the throne. As a young man, Saul had been the most handsome figure in Israel, a head taller than anyone else, a real head-turner among the young women (1 Sam. 9:2). God's Spirit had been with Saul. Soon, it would be David who would turn the ladies' heads. It would be David on whom God's favor rested. What Saul did not know was that God had already chosen David to replace him on the throne (1 Samuel 16).

Samuel the prophet had warned him that the day he turned his back on God's leading, he would be replaced. When David first entered Saul's service, he seemed to pose no threat. But Saul allowed into his household the very man who would contribute to his downfall. At first, Saul loved David greatly and promoted him to be his armor bearer (1 Sam. 16:21). The whole royal household fell in love with David—servants and all (1 Sam. 18:22). Saul's son Jonathan made David his blood brother and loved him as his own soul (1 Sam. 18:1–4). David called Saul "father," and Saul, in turn, addressed him as "son" (1 Sam. 24:11, 16). They became family for each other. And Michal watched him, this winsome young stud, her brother's best friend, who could calm her violent father and save the whole household from his evil-spirit-driven tantrums. David not only would be powerful on the battlefield, but he could knock out the evil presence that took hold of her father. David's presence brought a measure of peace for this family, who lived in fear of their father's rants. They did not know it, but David's ascent in the eyes of God and the people would also bring an end to any hopes this family had for building a dynasty.

Saul watched Michal watching David and everybody else falling under the sway of this young man's charm, and eventually David's lyre could no longer tame the storm within. Saul's rage began to foam and froth. He was no longer the center of attention, and he could not stand it. An old Cherokee once passed on wisdom to his grandson about the battle that goes on inside people, and it applies to Saul. He said, "My son, the battle is between two wolves. One is evil. It is Anger, Sorrow, Regret, Greed, Arrogance, Self-pity, Guilt, Resentment,

Inferiority, Dishonesty, False pride, Superiority and Ego. . . .
The other is good. It is Joy, Peace, Love, Hope, Serenity, Humility, Kindness, Benevolence, Empathy, Generosity, Truth,
Compassion, and Faith." The grandson thought about it for a
minute and then asked his grandfather, "Which wolf wins?"
The grandfather replied, "The one you feed." Saul fed the
"evil wolf," which grew ever more ravenous.

It takes a healthy person to love self and then to be able
to love others as much. Even more, it takes a sense of feeling secure in being loved to rejoice when those we love in
turn love others. It is that kind of security that parents need
to watch with joy as their children learn to love others. The
loving daddy knows he cannot forever be the center of his
daughter's affection if she is truly to grow into the full bloom
of adulthood. Moreover, it is simply the way the world works
that the parental generation controls things for a while and
then must give way for their children's generation to carry
on. Saul chafed over this reality. Instead of rejoicing in his
children's love for David, he simmered in a stew of jealousy
and rage.

When Michal expressed her love for David and took the
initiative of choosing her husband, she broke the cultural
convention that women were to be sought after; they did
not proclaim their love first. Moreover, she loved a man just
like her father—handsome, daring, charismatic—and prone
to self-importance, putting himself first over the needs of
others, even his family. Soon she would become the pawn
of both her father and her husband in a high-stakes game to
see who would rule the nation.

None of them knew what the future would hold. Saul, restive and churning with increasing fury, only intuited the trouble
lurking ahead. David saw an opportunity to advance his career
from this match with the king's daughter. Michal was oblivi-

ous, choosing to pledge her love to a partner without knowing whom he and she would become together. But then, none of us can know that. None of us can choose the "right" partner, the perfect one, since no such man or woman exists. Instead, love is a journey of mutual commitment into an unknown future. The most we can do is pledge to love one another as much as we love ourselves, to put the beloved first, to cherish one another. Sadly, Michal was to get none of that from the men in her life—not from her daddy, not from her beloved.

What's Love Got to Do with It? (1 Samuel 18:21–30)

Because of David's popularity and because "the Lord was with David but had departed from Saul" (1 Sam. 18:12), Saul now openly regarded David as the real menace to his hold on power. The little ditty sung by the women across Israel, "Saul has killed his thousands, and David his ten thousands" (1 Sam. 18:7), rang in Saul's ears and stoked his jealousy and resentment into a superheated inferno. The text tells us that Saul "eyed David from that day on" (1 Sam. 18:9). It was a jaundiced eye, filled with fear and loathing. Twice, he tried to pin David to the wall with a well-aimed spear, but David dodged the bullet, so to speak, each time (1 Sam. 18:11). Saul made David a commander in the army in hopes that he might fall in battle, but David returned with greater triumphs to greater acclaim. Saul offered David his daughter Merab if he would continue to fight valiantly the Lord's battles, still hoping that an intrepid Philistine warrior might bring him down. David pled humility and claimed he was unworthy to become the king's son-in-law, and so Merab went to another man (1 Sam. 18:17–19).

When he first learned of Michal's affection for David, Saul was pleased (1 Sam. 18:20), but for all the wrong reasons.

He was certainly not focused on Michal's happiness. Instead, he saw her love as presenting him with another window of opportunity to plot David's untimely end. He gave fulsome approval of his daughter's choice for a marriage partner and roared to David, "You shall now be my son-in-law!" all the while plotting how this betrothal would work to his own advantage to rid himself forever of this upstart. David had become too popular with the people simply to have him killed. Saul would use Michal as an unwitting accomplice to bring about the end to the very man she purposed to marry.

David, once again, pled his unworthiness and humble roots before the king, "Do you think it is a small matter to become the king's son-in-law? I'm only a poor man and little known" (1 Sam. 18:23, NIV). His self-effacement subtly implied that he did not have the means to pay an appropriate bride price for a king's daughter. Just the response Saul was counting on! The trap was sprung, and Saul offered a suitable alternative. "How about a special deal for you, David? My daughter in exchange for the foreskins of one hundred Philistines?" The odds were in Saul's favor. He thought he could count on at least one of those hundred Philistines killing David. David may have killed his myriads, but his luck was bound to run out someday. Philistines were hardly going to give up their foreskins voluntarily. As David says in Joseph Heller's satirical novel, *God Knows*, it was easiest to circumcise grown men "if you killed them first." No lone warrior, however brave and skilled, could hope to accomplish this feat unscathed. Saul had only agreed to the marriage because he never expected it to come to pass.

Saul was a true narcissist with a grandiose sense of self-importance. He required constant affirmation and could not stand for others to receive attention and accolades. He lacked empathy, even for his own children. His own future was more important to him than his daughter's. Michal was just an object to accomplish his own ends—dealing out death to David. He gave no thought to the grief his plan would cause Michal. He did not care that she would see herself as the cause of death for the man she loved—David would die trying to meet her father's demands to marry her.

Saul is such a horrible parent that some may actually find comfort reading about him and comparing their parenting to his. "At least," we might say to ourselves, "I'm not as bad a parent as Saul." Every parent makes mistakes; some are bigger mistakes than others. We may not be adequate to bring up our children, but that does not mean that they are ruined for life. We cannot forget the grace of God that somehow intervenes where we fail. Saul totally lacked empathy for others, but somehow he produced a caring, loving son like Jonathan. God worked through this inadequate, indifferent, irrational father. Jonathan was the exact opposite of his father. He became David's soul mate, a friend who loved beyond measure, who not only loved David but also risked his own life again and again for David's sake. When God works in our lives, even crazy parents can raise loving, compassionate, kind children.

Saul also raised a strong daughter. Over the past century, movies of this story, such as *David and Bathsheba*, have portrayed Michal as plain and drab, particularly in comparison to the stunning Bathsheba. They stereotype her as a shrew. There is no textual basis for such representations. The only thing we know is that there is precious little evidence that David returned her love. Perhaps it had more to do with David loving himself too much to love anybody else than with any failing in Michal. As India Edghill has Michal bitterly explain things in her novelized account of Michal's life, *Queenmaker*: "There are many who say that David loved me because I resembled my brother Jonathan. That is not true; David loved no woman, though he lay with many. Women loved him" (Edghill 2002).

David, like Saul, was a proud, self-absorbed man. Saul had counted on David's sense of honor to make him want to rise to the challenge of collecting the Philistine foreskins. David did not flinch or complain that the price was too high. It does not seem to have been his love for Michal that caused him to take Saul's challenge and risk his life to gain her as his wife. Perhaps his macho pride would not let him lose face by refusing such a challenge and thus besmirching his glory as a dauntless warrior. Reading between the lines, it also seems that David hoped to use Michal's love for him to achieve his own aspirations. He had his own ulterior reasons for agreeing to this union and the harrowing conditions attached to it. Just as it "pleased" Saul for Michal to love David because it served his interests, so "it pleased" David to be loved by a woman so well connected. This marriage would give him credibility with the royals and a firmer toehold in the halls of power. Perhaps he now became enamored with the idea of becoming the king's son-in-law and the power that position would provide (1 Sam. 18:26). It was a good career move to join the family's ruling business, and it was another step closer to the throne that Samuel had said would eventually become his (1 Sam. 16:1–13). For both men, Saul and David, Michal simply served as a means to attain their own self-centered ends and ambitions.

We might not be surprised when people "out in the world" treat us this way. The sales representatives appear to be friendly, but they are using their relational skills to drive the best deal for themselves. The boss is kind and provides job perks, but it is all a part of keeping the workforce happy and productivity up, and the boss won't hesitate to let us go when productivity slips. Coworkers seem to be friends and then stab us in the back when it suits them. We expect close family members to be different. Family members are supposed to look out for the well-being of one another, to care about one another, to hurt when we hurt—and certainly not to use us for their own selfish ends and deliberately hurt us. Child sexual abuse by a parent horrifies us because instead of protecting the child, the parent uses the child for self-gratification with no regard for the child's needs. Such behavior is the absolute opposite of the selfless love expected of a parent. A beloved partner or sibling is supposed to think about and to care about our needs. There is no worse betrayal than that of a spouse or a sibling who sells us out in order to gain some self-centered purpose.

To be fair, the Bible never actually says what David's motive was for taking the challenge and marrying Michal. He is the hero of the story, after all, and the narrator had no interest in portraying him negatively as an ambitious cad. The biblical heroes like David were like us, real flesh-and-blood characters who were fallible and feisty, with feet of clay. It is never the case that all the good guys are entirely good or the bad guys entirely evil. As in the story of Judah and Tamar and many other biblical stories, David is another biblical hero with jagged, broken edges who cuts things and leaves his imprint on history. David's jagged edges left an indelible mark on Israel, but they also cut Michal to the quick.

God anointed David and destined him to become king and have his name forever associated with the lineage of the Messiah, but David was flawed. It is safe to say that he was probably not a sensitive, gentle, considerate husband. The scriptures do not cover up his abuse of others to get what he wanted. Power is like the ring in J. R. R. Tolkien's *Lord of the Rings* that can bewitch even the best of persons as well as the worst. Power—seizing it, maintaining it, exercising it—becomes more important, and goodness is neglected. David was sinful, as are we all. And sin hurts not only sinners but also those who love them and a lot of innocent bystanders. Every family knows that from experience.

Perhaps Michal's motives were not as pure as the driven snow, either. If she cast her lot in with David and he became king, she would become the king's wife, and perhaps the lure of that position influenced her. We cannot know. But we can assume that her love for David may have been just as genuine as her brother Jonathan's love for him. David risks his life to marry her, and Michal will risk her life for him.

The Great Escape (1 Samuel 19)

Like the cartoon character Wile E. Coyote, who always fails to nab the Roadrunner despite his ingenious contraptions, Saul failed to destroy David with his demand for one hundred Philistine foreskins. David lived up to his reputation as a daredevil warrior, and he proudly, and perhaps somewhat haughtily, produced *double* the asking price—two hundred foreskins! David's men counted out the bloody bounty one by one in front of the king. In the distance, two hundred Philistine mothers wept when their sons' bodies were brought home, casualties in King Saul's horrific family power game. There is no word about either Saul or David consulting God in this bloody contest.

Saul had been foiled again and so had to give his daughter to his sworn enemy. What should have been the happy occasion of his youngest daughter's wedding became the springboard for renewed efforts to knock off his new son-in-law. Once again, Saul showed his total lack of care for Michal. He sent henchmen to kill David in his daughter's bed (1 Sam.

19:1). Michal somehow sensed danger, and she faced her moment of decision. She had to choose between her father and her husband. She chose David.

Michal lowered David through their bedroom window in a basket so that he could escape. She then gave him time to make his getaway with a cover story. "He is ill," she told her father's men. She used the old fake body-in-the-bed trick to fool his pursuers. Instead of plumped-up pillows under the covers, however, Michal placed a stone idol in her husband's side of the bed, with goats' hair at the head (1 Sam. 19:12). It must have looked like David had been down sick for a long time, with a bad case of "bed head" as the result. She fooled Saul's goons. What a nice Jewish girl like Michal was doing with an idol lying around the house, and a big one at that, is not explained. Ironically, this block of stone on David's side of the bed seemed to symbolize the kind of husband David would be for Michal.

On top of losing David, who fled into hiding to escape Saul's wrath, Michal was left to catch the full brunt of it. Saul thundered, "Why did you deceive me like this, and send my enemy away, so that he escaped?" She might have asked, "Why did you make my husband your enemy, and why are you trying to kill him?" Instead, she fibbed. There was no use arguing. Michal knew that her father's desires always trumped her own. She knew him and his violent temper all too well. So she submissively answered with a lie, "He said to me, 'Let me go. Why should I kill you?'" (1 Sam. 19:17, NKJV).

Rescue by Deception (Exodus 1:15–21)

It is not the first time that a powerful man dragged a woman before him, ordering her to defend her actions. In Egypt, long before Moses told Pharaoh that God commanded him, "Let my people go," Abraham's descendants had been "fruitful and multiplied greatly" (Exod. 1:7, NIV). They had become very strong people. The new pharaoh grew afraid of them, because they were so strong and so many. He decided to weaken them by turning them into slaves and to reduce their population explosion through controlled genocide. His method was heart-wrenching—have the midwives kill the boy babies as they were born and tell the mothers that their children were stillborn.

Shiphrah and Puah were poor slave midwives without families. They did not become midwives with the intention of becoming social revolutionaries, but revolutionaries they became. When one thinks of who is most likely to be the powerful shapers of history, one probably would not first think of slaves, or midwives, or even today's social workers, or schoolteachers, or store clerks—not people like us. Unlike the all-powerful Pharaoh, these women are named and become courageous heroines. It is ironic that we have to guess the identity of this pharaoh, but two humble women in traditional female professions are remembered in scripture. When faced with the pitiless decree of this powerful king, Shiphrah and Puah feared God more than they feared Pharaoh. They let the baby boys live. Imagine how they must have felt when they were hauled in front of Pharaoh and he bellowed, "Why have you done this? Why have you let the boys live?" They resorted to a lie. With all the innocence they could muster, they said, "Hebrew women are not like Egyptian women; they are vigorous and give birth before the midwives arrive" (Exod. 1:19, NIV); and Pharaoh believed this whopper that these women just popped those babies out. One of the baby boys they protected by risking their own lives was Moses, the one who would lead his people out from under this oppression.

Michal, too, protected the future leader of her people with her concocted story. We do not know what Saul would have done to her if she had told him that she had chosen to save David. Perhaps he would have speared her in his anger, as he had tried to spear David (see 1 Sam. 18:10–11; 19:9–10; 20:32–33).

Courage always means recognizing that what we may be called to do and need to do is bigger than the fear that holds us back. Courage means recognizing that what we are called to do is so important that we hope the leap of faith we make is stronger than the forces that will cause us to fall short. It means doing something even when we are afraid, even when we do not feel strong enough or wise enough. Shiphrah and Puah were strong and unwavering, cunning and creative in defending the children. Because of Shiphrah and Puah, the children lived. Because of Shiphrah and Puah, *Moses* had a chance to live long enough to be hidden by his mother, to be rescued by the princess, to become the rescuer of his people. When it was up to them, they put their own lives on the line for the sake of the children. Therefore, God was kind to the midwives and gave them "families of their own" (Exod. 1:21, NIV). Seemingly powerless, defenseless women put their fate in the hands of God and stepped out in faith to defend others. Few of us will be dragged before kings for history-shaping moments like these women faced, but all of us—men and women—shape history in one way or another, big and small, by our willingness to be courageous for the sake of what is right and good, to take leaps of faith when we are afraid, praying and believing that God is directing us and has hold of us.

How are we to make sense of lying as a means of furthering God's purposes? This God is not a God of simple rules: Always tell the truth. Be at church whenever the doors are open. Give 10 percent of your earnings. Then you can expect to be blessed. No, this God works far more mysteriously. We must be ruled by God and not by the rule book, and God must direct our lives if we are to participate in the grand plan that is being worked out through us, even when we have no idea what that plan is. This God expects us to look out for the well-being of others, to love them as we love ourselves, and to act on that love. For this God, caring for the well-being of others is the most important thing.

Pharaoh and Saul were both powerful men, with the ability to kill the women who defied them. These men were shameless, caring only for their own power and not for the families and children entrusted to their care as leaders. Shiphrah and Puah and Michal put themselves at great risk by pitting themselves against kings to protect those who were otherwise defenseless. Because of the midwives, the babies lived, and the Hebrew people eventually broke away from their slavery. Because of Michal, David lived to become the great ancestor of the Messiah. These women lived the promise of what family should be, to look out for the well-being of those we love, even when it costs us everything.

Saul was confounded by his daughter's betrayal of him, allowing her husband to escape his clutches. He could not fathom Michal's actions, because he thought he was the center of the world and did not know how anyone could love another so selflessly and loyally. Michal courageously risked her father's wrath to save David, just as her brother Jonathan had done (1 Sam. 19:1–6). She acted in true, sacrificial love, and it cost her. She stayed behind, confined behind the window through which she had lowered David, to face her father spitting with fury. Michal and David's parting words are not recorded. Did they vow undying love? Did he promise to come back for her?

Unlike Shiphrah and Puah, Michal received no blessing for her courage. Instead, she received only heartache. David never returned. He took other wives, Abigail and Ahinoam (1 Sam. 25:42–43), and later, he added four more. David continued to rendezvous with Jonathan and evidently loved his blood-brother/best friend more than his own wife (2 Sam. 1:26). The scriptures report that David loved Jonathan; nowhere does it say that David loved Michal.

Michal's words to her father had more meaning than she realized when she invented David's threat, "Why should I kill you?" She made her father think that David threatened to do her in if she did not help him beat a hasty retreat. In effect, it was the truth; David ended her life when he left her behind at the window where she abetted his getaway. She was stuck at home with an irate, irrational father, powerlessly waiting for a man who never returned. He deserted her.

David the Home Wrecker (2 Samuel 3:1–21)

Michal apparently did not get the chance to choose her mate again. It was Saul's prerogative to marry her off to whomever he chose, and he gave her to Paltiel (1 Sam. 25:44). As far as Saul was concerned, when David made tracks for the hills, it was a de facto divorce. Her marriage to Paltiel introduces the next scene, which is all about David, not Michal. Michal had no choice and is given no speaking part to voice her views.

David had gained the upper hand over Saul and was now reigning as king, but he was bedeviled by the unrest of the northern tribes who remained loyal to Saul. With Saul's daughter at his side, he thought, these northern tribes might come into line. Saul's line would become united with David's line, giving the offspring of their union more legitimacy as the son of a king and the grandson of a king. Michal was caught again in the net of David's political aims.

In negotiations with the weakening leaders of the house of Saul, David demanded that Saul's daughter, the wife he earned by the price of two hundred Philistine foreskins, be brought to him. The emphasis is on her being Saul's daughter, which implies that he was interested in her only for her political significance. David was simply consolidating his power, not returning to his first wife, a woman who loved him so much that she risked her own life to help him escape the wrath of her father. David now had six other wives and six sons by them (2 Sam. 3:2–5). The demand for Michal's return was driven only by political expediency.

Ishbaal, last surviving son of Saul, betrayed his own sister by snatching Michal from the arms of her new husband, Paltiel, in a feeble attempt to appease David. Paltiel pitifully followed after her abductors for a long distance, weeping all the way and hoping against hope that they would let her go. Clearly, he loved her. But Paltiel's love could not conquer David's imperial determination to reclaim Michal as a member of his ever expanding harem of wives. It is impossible to explain why people experience such enormous sorrows or why a happy marriage can be ripped to shreds by the callous selfishness of another. It only serves as further evidence that we live in a sinful, dying world that needs redemption. And that redemption will not come from an earthly king. What happened to Paltiel fulfilled the prophet Samuel's warning to the Israelites about the dangers of wanting a king rather than to be ruled by God (1 Sam. 8:11–18). Earthly rulers use their power to take what they want, and God will not answer the cries of the people when they have chosen to be so ruled. David's action was unlawful; the Mosaic law was clear that when a man divorces a woman—and David had abandoned Michal—he cannot take her again as his wife

(Deut. 24:1–4). It was this very threat of a former husband wrecking a second family that the law sought to address.

We are not told how Michal felt about her abduction. Was she snatched from her husband's arms in tears? Did she gouge her fingernails into the thugs who were sent to snatch her away? Did she go weeping silently, or did she wail over her shoulder to her forlorn husband? She could hardly be looking forward to returning to David. Perhaps she succumbed in numbed silence. She was now a helpless pawn in the hands of powerful men who were jockeying for power. The text robs her of any cry or emotion, and it seems that no one would have answered her cries anyway. It is clear that David's behavior is horrendous—steamrolling over the rights and feelings of others to further his own selfish agenda. It says nothing of their reunion. Michal had saved David's life, allowing him to steal away into the night. In return, he stole her away from her new life that seemed to promise happiness with a loving but powerless husband. It was not the last time that David would steal the wife of another man, a woman helpless to defend herself or her husband's honor when faced with the demands of the king. If the movies present her as a shrew, she certainly had good reason to grow bitter. She had been deeply wronged by politically motivated men who were supposed to love her—as a daughter, as a wife.

At the Dance (2 Samuel 6:12–23)

The last scene in which Michal appears in David's story reveals that a lot of water had passed under the bridge since she had announced her love for David (1 Sam. 18:20). David was bringing the recaptured ark of the Lord into the city of David, and he was greeted by a giant pep rally of excited people. The ark was just a box, but it symbolized God's presence among the people promising well-being, protection, and, for David, the legitimacy of his reign. David may have been filled with trepidation, remembering well what happened when he first tried to bring the ark back to Jerusalem. The oxen pulling the cart carrying the ark jostled it, and when a man named Uzzah reached out to steady it, immediately he was struck dead. The sight of Uzzah dropping in a dead heap beside the ark in the midst of the celebration froze everyone with horror, and David halted the procession and decided to house this fearsome, holy object somewhere far away from him—at the home of one his soldiers, Obed-edom the Gittite (2 Sam. 6:1–11). When he learned that the ark's presence had not laid waste the household of Obed-edom but had blessed it, he took that as an all clear to bring it back to the capital. His excitement knew no bounds as he returned once again as the conquering hero with the symbol of God's presence. There was a ticker-tape parade with mass mania, cheering, dancing, trumpets, and feasting. David led the festivities, leaping and breaking into a frenzied dance before the ark. Every six steps with the ark, the procession stopped, and they sacrificed a bull and a fattened calf. This time, it was a royal barbeque welcomed by God.

Once again, a window factors in the story. Michal had abetted David's escape through the window, and she now looked out at the celebration from behind a window. The window is a symbol of her confinement and inability to control her destiny. She looked out with a curled lip of disdain at her husband the king cavorting, in her jaundiced view, like a wild animal before the ark (2 Sam. 6:16). She was expected to stay behind the window in the house—to stay inside, be silent, and show discretion. But what she saw from the window was more than she could take, and she despised David in her heart. As Saul's daughter, she now eyed him the way her father had eyed him—with love turned to hatred. He was dancing before the

Lord, but she saw it only as prancing before the females in the crowd. Carried away in his enthusiasm, he had something akin to a wardrobe malfunction; he was half-naked. Michal thought he was trolling for more sexual conquests. After all, he had already taken six other wives while he had been on the run from Saul, leaving Michal abandoned (2 Sam. 3:2–5). While David frolicked bare-skinned in the warm sunshine, Michal was shut up inside. Her gaze, which started the story, has changed from desire to absolute contempt.

David's frenzy, free spirit, and lack of attire was not the only issue that sparked her fury. It had been smoldering for some time, and this incident caused it to burst into a firestorm. Robert Atler writes:

> The scorn for David welling up in Michal's heart is thus plausibly attributable in some degree to all of the following: the undignified spectacle which David is just now making of himself; Michal's jealousy over the moment of glory David is enjoying while she sits alone, a neglected co-wife, back at the provisional palace; Michal's resentment over David's indifference to her all these years, over the other wives he has taken, over being torn away from the devoted Paltiel; David's dynastic ambitions—now clearly revealed in his establishing the Ark in the 'City of David'—which will irrevocably replace the house of Saul. (Alter 1981, 123)

We do more harm to ourselves and to others when we view what happens in life through the colored lenses of our past pain.

Perhaps Michal also saw glimpses of her father in David. After she had covered for David and helped him to escape from her bedroom that terrible night, Saul sent men to capture David. But God protected him. God's Spirit overcame Saul's men, and they all began to have a spiritual camp meeting with David and Samuel. Saul followed in exasperation to do the evil deed himself, only to be caught up in the prophesying. He stripped off his clothing and lay naked in public all day and all night (1 Samuel 18–23).

Now Michal saw David leaping and dancing in the spirit and scantily clad, with no sense of royal dignity. He was hosting this incredible barbeque, playing to the people like her father had, and getting away with it. She had risked her life to save him from her father, only for him to become like her father. At least, that may have been the way she saw things.

David had wronged her, and he would wrong her again. He was a sinful man. But he was not her father. She was too wounded to see that David's joy was for the Lord, not for the women who were watching. He stripped down and danced because God was with him, and he understood it to be his self-humiliation before the Lord. He was not defeated like her father, but victorious. He would go on to achieve more victories, doing "what was just and right for all his people" (2 Sam. 8:15, NIV), not serving himself as her father had.

Michal's pent-up anger exploded in indignation, and she indiscreetly stepped out of the house to confront him. Here is the assertive Michal we knew at the beginning of the story, willing to step out in love then, in loathing now. David had humiliated himself publicly by what was in her eyes vulgar behavior, and she now spitefully attempted to shame him for this unkingly spectacle. It is the only dialogue that is ever recorded between them. Michal used biting sarcasm, "How the king of Israel honored himself today, uncovering himself before the eyes of his servants' maids, as any vulgar fellow might shamelessly uncover himself!" (2 Sam. 6:20). Notice the cold disdain in the use of the third person rather than the personal "you"—"The king of Israel has humiliated himself. He has embarrassed me. He has embarrassed God." There is no love in her words, no respect, no concern for him, no desire to give him queenly advice to help him. She uses her anger to attempt to tear him down in public. She has allowed her anger to carry her into sin.

David had come home exuberant. He had blessed the people "in the name of LORD Almighty" (2 Sam. 6:18) and sent them home. And at long last, he came home to Michal, who had waited so long. He came to bless his household, but she stopped him cold with her belittling sarcasm. David's blessing evaporated before it was ever spoken. Most husbands and wives do not appreciate being dressed down in public by their spouses for their shortcomings and gaffes. David's response ignores the substance of Michal's critique, and, as so many of us sadly do when attacked in a family fuss, he adds fuel to the flames. He went straight for the jugular and lashed out by bringing up the most painful event in her life, God's rejection of her father, and his subsequent death, along with three of Michal's brothers, at the hands of the Philistines. He rubbed salt in this old wound by rashly proclaiming, "It was before the LORD, who chose me in place of your father and all his household, to appoint me as prince over Israel, the people of the LORD, that I have danced before the LORD. I will make myself yet more contemptible than this, and I will be abased in my own eyes; but by the maids of whom you have spoken, by them I shall be held in honor" (2 Sam. 6:21–22). What he is saying is, "You belong to a royal line that God has cut off! I am God's Chosen One! How dare you challenge me! I am better than all of you—your father, even your beloved brother Jonathan!" Hints of her father's old cloven-hoofed, narcissistic self-centeredness emerge. "It is I whom the Lord has chosen. I am the Lord's chosen!" he crowed.

The ability to control what we say when we are angry is a precondition for any lasting marriage relationship, and both Michal and David had let fly with their cruelest barbs. David shrugged off the lifelong sacrifice Michal made to save him from certain death at her father's hands. He gave no acknowledgment that her brother Jonathan had selflessly protected him all his life, even when Jonathan, by doing so, ensured that David rather than he would take the throne. David, the handsome, valiant, spirit-filled warrior had lost all humility. He seemed to think that God had chosen him because he deserved it. Yet none of us deserves the blessing of God.

David's boast was portentous, because he indeed would make himself more contemptible with his sexual abuse of Bathsheba, robbing another husband of his wife. And he would take the fatal step of murdering the wronged husband to cover up his crime. Many have not seen it so, however. In the movie *David and Bathsheba*, after David and Michal had this quarrel, David immediately went out on the roof to cool off. It was then that he spied Bathsheba. In this interpretation, David was driven to the presumably more sensual Bathsheba by Michal's cold-eyed spite. The text does not support this presentation. Michal was right to warn David that he should learn from her father's downfall because of pride and self-importance. But her criticism did not carry the same weight with her husband as did the prophet Nathan's when he later confronted him about Bathsheba and the murder of her husband. Michal could not rebuke her husband the king in public with impunity.

Michal would never bear children (2 Sam. 6:23). Whether or not it was because David refused to be with her after this last exchange, we can only guess. Her childlessness solved a dynasty problem that occupied the narrator of the story in 1–2 Samuel. The line of Saul had reached a dead end. No descendant of Saul would ever take the throne again. Jonathan had been killed. Ishbaal has been killed—beheaded (2 Sam. 4:5–8). Michal was in David's stable of wives but would have no children by him. It must have become clear to her that she was simply a piece on the board of political gamesmanship. She had been used by her father, Saul, her brother Ishbaal, and her husband David. She was taken away from a husband who loved her and sequestered in the house of a husband who had six other wives and children by them, while she remained unloved and barren. She was a survivor, but it meant that she had to watch the house of Judah trample her family's line in the dust.

Bitterness Breeds Bitterness

Michal is a tragic figure. Her inability to forgive David leaves her sullen, joyless, and resentful. Would David have blessed her, loved her, if she had been willing to accept that blessing? Had *he* repented of abandoning her, leaving her to her father's mercy, then wrecking her second chance of happiness with a man who loved her? We do not know. David was a man who could repent—he would do so when confronted by Nathan after his sin with Bathsheba. But whether or not he repented of hurting Michal is not for us to know.

Michal seems an innocent victim. Her suffering is the story of so many women manipulated by power-hungry men, and it defies easy answers. Michal's name is a contraction of *Michael*, which translates to "who is like God?" From her story, we may wonder, indeed, what God is like. We do not always understand what God is doing—not then and not now. Perhaps we are not meant to understand, because we do not have God's perspective. That is why we must depend on God, we must keep listening for God's guiding. We practice forgiveness even when we are deeply angry and hurt and unsure of what it will bring in others.

Jesus simply commanded us to forgive. He did not promise that everything would then be made right, that our forgiveness will be met with humble repentance and glad restoration with those we forgive. We simply are expected to forgive, to be perfect as God in heaven is perfect. Forgiveness is not a get-happy-quick strategy for a more fulfilling life. Will Willimon observes: "It is in the nature of God to forgive, because God's forgiveness is built into the foundation of the world, because, in forgiving we . . . witness to the reign of God who is forgiveness" (Willimon 1998, 60).

When Michal complained about David making a spectacle of himself before all the girls with his "dirty dancing," he boasted that he would make himself more contemptible than this. It may have been bitter consolation for Michal that this boast would ironically come true. He would commit infamous acts, and his family would begin to fall apart. But if it did offer solace, it was a solace that gave no real comfort. It would be a sign that her soul had become as barren as her womb. It takes both repentance and forgiveness to reconcile a relationship after such a wounding experience, but we are called to forgive even when the relationship will never be restored. Forgiveness is a struggle; it is not easy to wish good rather than harm for those who have harmed us. Yet that is what Jesus called us to do. Otherwise, the hatred, the spite, the nursing of old wounds robs us of any future joy. Forgiveness does not mean that we forget the past, nor do we excuse the harm done us by an impenitent other. It does not mean we are not angry for the harm done. But it does mean refusing to allow the past to ruin our future. It means not allowing painful memories to keep us from living into the promises of a future. It means not allowing hatred and vindictiveness to prevail and permeate our lives. And if the other meets our forgiveness with repentance, it can mean restoration of shared love.

What would have happened if Michal had met David's joy with joy? If she had loved him, even though he had deserted her? If she had left a window open for him to come through with sorrow for his neglect of her? We will never know.

6

Bathsheba's Story

Surviving Abuse and Devastating Loss

2 Samuel 11:1–4a

Military exploits had garnered David great success. After a long struggle with Saul, David had finally become king, and now he could take it easy. The way the Bible states it leads the reader to think David may have grown soft and accustomed to the comforts of home rather than the rigors of battle: "In the spring of the year, the time when kings go out to battle, David sent Joab with his officers and all Israel with him; they ravaged the Ammonites, and besieged Rabbah. But David remained at Jerusalem" (2 Sam. 11:1). The assumption behind this notice is that kings make war and that they do so in the spring. David seemed to have lost his fighting edge. He was no longer the lion-hearted military adventurer of derring-do whose strong arm had vanquished Goliath and who had later presented King Saul with a string of Philistine foreskins as the bride price for Michal. David sent his troops off to do battle and stayed home, becoming an armchair general, lolling about on his roof enjoying the breeze, and, it seems, the scenery below. Spring is also the time when, proverbially, sexual passion rises.

From his rooftop vista, David spied a beautiful woman bathing. Artists and interpreters over the centuries have turned this particular woman into a painted sex kitten who bewitched a divinely chosen king. They accuse her of deliberately choosing to bathe in a place where she knew she could be seen by the king. They imagine her coquettishly parading around naked to catch the king's eye. As a consequence of this portrayal of the scene, David seems almost a helpless victim in the sights of a conniving vixen determined to seduce him. Since David is identified as a man after the Lord's "own heart" (1 Sam. 13:14), God's chosen one ("the LORD was with him," 1 Sam. 18:14), it is hard to imagine that he could sin without some tantalizing temptress making him do it. We need someone to blame for our hero's fall. Artists and movies have therefore contorted the biblical story, leading us to believe that David was dazzled by a gold-digging, bathing belle intent on arousing his desire so as to ensnare him.

The 1951 movie *David and Bathsheba* is such a portrayal. David, played by Gregory Peck, confesses to Bathsheba, played by Susan Hayward, how much he desires her. He scoffs at how stupid her husband, Uriah, is to prefer the stink of battle to the intoxicating perfume of his beautiful wife. He huffs, "He has no blood, no heart." Otherwise, David implies, Uriah would desire her as much as he does and would want to spend every moment he could with her—instead of only six days in the last seven months. David then warns Bathsheba that he would like to ravish her like a king who can take whatever he wants: "Be thankful that I'm not Pharaoh. At least I can console myself with the thought that your modesty matches your beauty." Bathsheba responds coyly: "Perhaps you would prefer truth to modesty, sire. Before you went away, I used to watch you every evening as you walked on your terrace. Always at the same hour, always alone. Today I heard you had returned."

David: "And you knew that I . . . ."

Bathsheba: "You'd be on your terrace tonight? Yes. I had heard that never had the king found a woman to please him. I dared to hope I might be that woman."

David: "Why are you telling me this now? Why not before?"

Bathsheba: "Because, first I had to know what was in your heart. If the law of Moses is to be broken, David, let us break it in full understanding of what we want from each other" (Gunn 1996, 98).

Taking remarkable license with the story, the screen writers changed Bathsheba from the one who is ogled by David into David's stalker. She is the femme fatale who initiates things, knowing full well what she wants and what the consequences will be. She takes the role of Satan: "Let's break the law of Moses, and let's do it with gusto." The result of this portrayal is that David appears to be victimized by a cunning woman and is hardly responsible for what happened. Who wants to see Gregory Peck as a sexual predator? He is bewitched by an enchantress and betrayed by his own male virility and Uriah's lack of virility.

It is simply male fantasy to think that women are being seductive when they are in fact being exploited (Rutter

1989, 69). It is not surprising, then, that the movie *David and Bathsheba*, written, directed and produced by males, makes the cinematic Bathsheba conform to male fantasies about women. A steamy seductress enticing a king with her feminine charms sells movies, but the text does not support this reading. For example, it does not mention *how* she is bathing. She is not taking a bubble bath or lounging in a hot tub. The law required ritual washing at the conclusion of her menstrual period. A woman would be highly unlikely to conduct such a cleansing from her menstrual period as a come-on. If she were in public view, she would have washed without disrobing. There is no reason even to assume that she was naked. Public nudity was not acceptable in this ancient Jewish culture but instead was considered shameful. There is no foundation for assuming she was some kind of exhibitionist. Ila Marie Davis, a former missionary in Morocco, makes an observation about rooftops in that culture that probably applied also in David's time and makes his conduct all the more blameworthy:

> Rooftops are the women's domain, a safe place where they can be outdoors, do the laundry, bathe, relax with embroidery and gossip with other women on adjoining rooftops. Men are not allowed to look down on a neighbor's roof. No one could look down on ours, at any rate. Our house loomed far above any others around us, and our rooftop walls were very high. Missionaries living at Derb Skat got into trouble once, though. Because the rooms were windowless, one group of missionaries decided to build a window high up on the twenty-foot wall. Unfortunately, it overlooked someone's roof. Soon neighbors came over to complain, asking the missionaries to close the window. It is boarded up to this day. (Davis and Stenbock-Ditty, 1998, 32)

Male-dominated cultures like Bathsheba's and our own teach women that they are responsible for men's lust. Women may think and may have been told that their behavior evokes this response in men—somehow they have telegraphed availability messages. As a consequence, when men lust after them, some women feel guilty. Somehow, they think they have caused the sexual harassment, the unwanted sexual come-ons or touching, or even the rape. Others may suggest to an abused woman that it was because of the way she dressed or carried herself or looked at a man—or maybe she should not have been where she was in the first place. Not only must women cope with what is done to them, but then they are blamed for causing the harassment or abuse. Bathsheba exemplifies how unjust it is to assign responsibility for male lust to the woman. Bathsheba had done nothing for which she should bear guilt; David had invaded her privacy.

David, not Bathsheba, is the subject of all the action described: He rises from bed, walks around, sees, sends, and inquires. Bathsheba was only the eroticized object of his lust and sexual fantasy. David did not even know who this beautiful woman was, suggesting that they had never met. The text identifies her. She was a person with a name, Bathsheba. She was someone's daughter—Eliam's, who, if he is the same Eliam who is mentioned in 2 Samuel 23:34, was one of David's valiant warriors in a group known as "the Thirty" and the son of his close adviser Ahitophel (2 Sam. 16:23). She was someone's wife, Uriah's, who was off fighting David's war. None of this information deterred David. He did not care about Bathsheba as a person; to him, she was only a beautiful object to possess, another conquest. David was pleased to receive the kingdom of Israel as a gift from God. Now as the king, he takes whatever he pleases, including another man's wife. He looked down on her in more ways than one—literally from his rooftop vista above her, and from his position of power over her. The gaze of a powerful man packs power. E. Ann

Kaplan remarks that "men do not simply look; their gaze carries with it the power of action and of possession which is lacking in the female gaze. Women receive and return a gaze, but cannot act upon it" (Kaplan 1983, 31). Bathsheba had no opportunity to return David's first gaze. She did not even know that she was in David's sights. She was defenseless and clueless that she had become an object of a powerful man's desire to possess. She was simply kindling that ignited the flames of his passion, not a person with a name and a family and a life of her own.

David was king; he had covenantal responsibility for the well-being of his people, including and perhaps especially Bathsheba, since her husband was off fighting David's war. One wonders if David's lustful gaze was accidental? Was it happenstance that he was on the roof at the time she was cleansing herself? Or, was he on the roof trolling, so to speak, for sexual conquests? The text does not tell us. The result of his gaze, however, is clear and disastrous. The look led to desire; desire to intent; intent to pursuit; and pursuit to deed. Bathsheba was the victim of a man with authority, the leader of his people, abusing his power—something akin to employer sexual harassment or clergy sexual abuse today. David was violating his covenant responsibility as the God-ordained king of the nation.

Everyone wants to believe that they have the power to make decisions and act on them; no one wants to feel helpless or out of control of their lives. But when someone who has power over us and whom we trust is manipulating us, even our ability to sort out right from wrong is confused. Abusers play up the power differential, increasing their power and the victim's helplessness. David did not try to meet Bathsheba on neutral ground, in at least some attempt to treat her as an equal. Quite the contrary, not only did he send for her rather than going to her himself, he increased his power (her even more by sending multiple messengers to fetch her (2 Sam. 11:4). It was a power move that could not be refused. She could not respond, "Oh, I'm too busy to answer the king." She must have been so frightened by this summons; what could the king want from her? In thinking about this sudden request, the only reason for David to summon her that made any sense would be to tell her that her husband had been killed in battle. What else could it be? Refusal to answer David's summons was unthinkable. She had never met the king. He was known as the chosen of God; she would not have imagined that he was calling on her for sexual favors. Nothing could have prepared her for what was to come.

Abuse of Power: The Rape (2 Samuel 11:4b)

The description of Bathsheba in 2 Samuel 11:3 as "Uriah's wife" marks her as off limits even to a king. But the next verse begins with a surprising "so." "So," David had her fetched to him. Presumably, David believed no one was off limits to him and that he could wield his power to have whatever and whomever he wanted, even the wife of a neighbor, a loyal servant, and his soldier fighting his war. Bathsheba had no reason not to trust David; he was the God-appointed king for whom her husband was risking his life. All Israel loved David, and he was known for doing what was "just and right for all his people" (2 Sam. 8:15). She was his subject, and she knew his sterling reputation as God's appointed leader, a man purportedly just and righteous. She did not know about the vermin crawling around beneath the floorboards of his religious facade and reputation. She did not know that he was capable of stooping so low as to trap and use her to satisfy his burning lusts. The setup was complete. By acquiescing to go with the king's messengers, suddenly she found herself in a compromising position, alone with the king. Who would believe her should she accuse him of any wrongdoing? It was her word against his, and he was the great king. She was only a woman. There was no escape.

Most interpreters of this story have ignored the inherent power differential between a king and one of his female subjects, and this king was invested not only with political power but also with spiritual power. The power differential between King David and Bathsheba is clear from an interchange between them at the end of David's life. Bathsheba was again summoned into his presence, and she bowed and did obeisance to the king (1 Kings 1:16) and called him "my lord the king" (1 Kings 1:20). Later, in her last appearance before David, again she bowed with her face to the ground, did obeisance to the king, and said, "May my lord King David live for ever!" (1 Kings 1:31). She had been by then his wife for many years, presumably his favorite wife. If she was this deferential after all these years of intimacy, imagine how she must have felt when she first was ushered into his presence. The saucy flirtation with David that the movies imagine and dramatize has no basis in the story.

David was in total control of the situation, even to the point that he may have twisted her into believing that she agreed to lie with him. He was a powerful manipulator. She must have been terribly anxious, to be fetched into the presence of the king with no idea what his agenda actually was. Anxiety would have heightened her confusion and emotions, whatever they were. Perhaps she was flattered by his attention. He was a handsome man; perhaps she found herself attracted to him. Even if she was flattered by the attention of the king, however, and even if she found him attractive, she was not responsible for what happened. Since consent was impossible, given her powerless position, David in essence raped her. Rape means to have sex against the will, without the consent, of another—and she did not have the power to consent. Even if there was no physical struggle, even if she gave in to him, it was rape. The narrator does not count it important enough even to comment on Bathsheba's feelings, or whether she fought unsuccessfully to escape him. It is not important because regardless of what she felt or did or didn't do, the narrator does not hold her responsible. David planned it, he used all of his power to manipulate her into a situation impossible to escape, and he raped her. Then he sent her away. The encounter is only half a verse. In half a verse, her whole world changed.

"Then she returned to her house" (2 Sam. 11:4b). What must she have felt like, pulling her clothing around her, walking out of his bed chamber, through the palace, and home? Did she pass the king's servants, or the messengers who had brought her to the king? What did they say to her, or did they just stare at her? What knowing looks were cast behind her? Shame flamed on her face. Perhaps she was going over and over in her mind how she could have let this happen, blaming herself. Perhaps David had told her that he had watched her, implying that what happened was her own fault for not realizing she was in his view. She would be inclined to believe this powerful man, because there was no one else who could help her sort out what she had been through. How could she let this happen? A question that often helps women who have been abused by a man in power is, "Would this have happened if he were your neighbor and not your king/boss/pastor?" Almost always, the answer is "no." No, because then she would have had her own power and ability to say no. Bathsheba lay with David not because she wanted to, but because she could do nothing to stop him. If she realized her powerlessness, that too made her feel ashamed.

Sexual abuse is inherently shaming. Any time one person treats another as an object to be used to gratify needs rather than as an "Other," worthy of respect, the user shames the one used (Horst 1998). This shaming is accentuated when the abuser is a spiritual leader, as David was. Because he had redefined what was right based on his own needs as the God-appointed king, she may have been left questioning her own ability to distinguish right from wrong. David showed no remorse for what he had done. If this is a king that does justice for *all* his people, then what was this? So she walked home, blamed and shamed. And that shame and blame has continued to be heaped on her throughout the centuries.

At a social gathering last winter, a woman who works in a crisis pregnancy program with teenagers began talking to us about a Bible study curriculum that she has used with teenagers that has a title something like "Naughty Girls of the Bible." "You know," she said, "women like Rahab and Bathsheba. Prostitutes and adulteresses." When we suggested that perhaps the label "adulteress" does not fit Bathsheba, that Bathsheba was instead a victim of abuse of power, the woman was stunned. Then she began pondering out loud. "You are right; how could she say no to the king?" Then she said with some shock, "Why haven't I ever thought about her in this way?" The response, of course, is that too often it is only men in power who read the Bible to us. Biblical scholars have identified a common theme in the stories about struggles over kingly succession: "the woman who brings death" (Gunn 1978, 43). That may be a literary theme, but in real life it is further victimizing the victim by blaming her rather than seeking justice for her. The woman has done nothing wrong; she is simply being beautiful and vulnerable. It is sin that brings death, and the sin is David's.

Even if Bathsheba had not been someone's wife, she was a person created in God's image. When Jesus condemned sexual lust, he denied the right of the man to sexual freedom on the basis that the woman, whether she is someone's wife or not, is a person who is on the same level and possesses the same dignity as the man: "You have heard that it was said, 'You shall not commit adultery.' But I say to you that every one who looks at a woman with lust has already committed adultery with her in his heart" (Matt. 5:27–28). Adulterous looks, Jesus made clear, are sins against her, not just against her husband.

The English translation here creates some problems. In Greek, the verb "to lust" and the verb "to commit adultery" can take direct objects; they are actions done to another. English idiom requires that we render it "commits adultery *with* her." The English idiom thus implies some complicity on the woman's part when there is none. The woman is simply being lusted after. The Greek idiom more readily expresses the problem that Jesus was trying to correct. The man "lusts" her (direct object) and "adulterates" her. In other words, the lustful look dehumanizes the woman. She is reduced to an object for the male's sexual gratification. Sexual sins are a self-centered exploitation of others. The verb "to lust" in Greek is the same verb form that is often translated "to covet." In English, we can speak of a lust for power and lust for gold with the implicit idea of gaining possession of them. Sexual fantasizing sees the other person in a one-dimensional role as some "thing" that one can possess, use, and then discard. Indeed, this is what happened in David's encounter with Bathsheba. He sent for her, had sex with her, and then sent her away. He used her and discarded her.

"Sending for" and "taking" are what kings do. When Abraham was sojourning in a foreign land, he feared for his life because of the beauty of his wife, Sarah. Someone might kill *him* to get his hands on her, he selfishly worried. So, he passed off his wife as his sister. King Abimelech of Gerar did what kings do; he "sent and took Sarah" (Gen. 20:2). This rule of might is exactly what Samuel had forewarned would happen when Israel insisted on getting a human king. These are the ways of a king, Samuel protested: He will reign over you, and then "he will take your sons . . . ; he will take your daughters . . . ; he will take one-tenth of your grain and of your vineyards . . . ; he will take your male and female slaves . . . ; he will take one-tenth of your flocks. . . . And in that day you will cry out . . . but the LORD will not answer you" (1 Sam. 8:11–19). In effect, Samuel warns, "You made your bed; you will have to lie in it."

Unfortunately, it is a bed that women will have to lie in as well, and against their will. Bathsheba was the object of aggression. David had taken other wives for himself—including another man's wife that he thought he had some right to because he had married her, even though he then abandoned her (Michal, who had been married to Paltiel). He now took another man's wife he *knew* was rightfully not his. The law echoes Samuel's warning about the way with kings: "And he must not acquire many wives for himself, or else his heart will turn away; also silver and gold he must not acquire in great quantity for himself" (Deut. 17:17). David went beyond what Samuel feared would happen. He acquired a passel of wives, including the wives of other men—three times, Abigail, Michal, and now, Bathsheba.

Bathsheba was sent for and was taken. This was no sexual affair. An affair assumes mutual consent, and there was no indication—or even possibility for—consent. The two did not see each other or have sex again until Uriah was dead and David took her as his wife. There was no relationship; he tossed her aside.

How could she ever explain what had happened to her husband? In fact, she has never been allowed to explain what happened. She has no voice in the text to cry out her innocence, so that throughout the centuries she has been perceived as a guilty accomplice in sin. She has been seen as "committing adultery" with David. Her portrayal in the movies and popular imagination compounds the injustice of her rape by making her a seductress rather than a victim of the king's abuse. The fallout spreads to innocent and guilty alike. Though guiltless, the victim suffers punishment. Had her husband Uriah lived to find out about it, he probably would have never been able look at her in the same way again, even if he tried to understand things from her perspective.

Perhaps, since David is a biblical hero, readers want to clear him of any unscrupulous behavior. The rationalization is that David was going through a midlife crisis. He had grown weary of the battles that marked his kingship and was leaving the fighting to others. All of his multiple marriages were unfulfilling. One can imagine him excusing himself: "My wives are so cold; they do not understand me" or "The duties of my office are so heavy; I am a great man with great needs that need to be met if I am to continue to serve my people well." The narrator of this story, however, drops enough clues to expose David's sinfulness, though he had no intention of dealing with the issues that we are attending to in this chapter. The verbs describing what David did are telling: He saw, he sent, he took, and he lay.

The frightening aspect of this story is that David was known as a man after God's own heart, a "good" man. Our world is full of such "good" men. This is not just some ancient story; it is a story repeated over and over today. Abuse of power happens in schools, in the workplace, and in the church, when people have opportunity to use and abuse others because they have the power to do so and there are no protective safeguards in place. Our families and our communities are home to those who have been victims of these "good" men who use the perception of their goodness to manipulate carelessly and abuse others. As we can see from Bathsheba's story, expecting potential victims to "just say no" and stand up for themselves is not a realistic strategy for preventing leaders from abusing their power. Nor can we assume that it is only "bad people" who unleash evil in their lives and the lives of others. Perhaps even more dangerous are "good" men with unchecked power over others.

Hiding Evil with Evil (2 Samuel 11:5–27)

The little detail that Bathsheba was purifying herself from her uncleanness, her menstrual period (2 Sam. 11:4), is a critical one for the story. Her bathing was part of her ritual cleansing from her menstruation (see Lev. 15:19–24; and McCarter 1984, 286; Halpern 2001, 35). It establishes David's paternity for the baby that was now growing in her womb. She was not pregnant before David had sex with her. Her husband, Uriah, was still at the battlefront when she was impregnated. Only David could be the father of this child. There is no indication that David desired her to become his wife. Otherwise, why did he take such pains to try to get Uriah back home so that he could be assumed to be the father? Presumably, he wanted the marriage of Uriah and Bathsheba to continue. He just wanted to steal Uriah's wife for a moment of pleasure for himself.

Bathsheba sent word to David, actually two words: "I'm pregnant!" This message is the only action she takes that is recorded in this episode. The narrator does not record her inflection, but one can bet it was not an exclamation of joy. Little did she know that her words would seal her husband's doom. She remained a naive victim. She could not have imagined what the king would do when he summoned her. She also could not have imagined what he would do when he heard these words. She was trapped and desperate.

David plotted alone, the face of evil becoming rapidly more sinister. He continued to wield power over Bathsheba, neither consulting nor comforting her, much less expressing any remorse at what he had done to her. He decided to call Uriah home from the front on the pretense of gathering information about how the battle was going and also giving a battle-weary soldier a chance for some rest and relaxation—and to sleep in his own bed. He invited him, perhaps with a wink, to go home and "wash his feet," a euphemism for sexual intercourse (2 Sam. 11:8). Then, when a baby arrived on the scene nine months later, no one would be the wiser.

David's scheme failed. Uriah was too good for his own good. Uriah did not think or act the way David did, who appears to have been driven by desire to do what he wanted without regard for the cost to others. Uriah, of Gentile ancestry—identified seven times as a "Hittite" in case the dense reader might miss it the first time—had a sense of duty and honor that put the king of Israel to shame. His loyalty to his comrades in arms foiled David's plan. He refused to go home to the comfort of his own bed and wife, and declared: "The ark and Israel and Judah remain in booths; and my lord Joab and the servants of my lord are camping in the open field; shall I then go to my house, to eat and to drink, and to lie with my wife? As you live, and as your soul lives, I will not do such a thing" (2 Sam. 11:11). No cajoling on David's part would cause him to yield and break the unwritten code of solidarity with his band of brothers. Uriah would take cold showers and do push-ups and would not go in to his wife while his companions were slogging away in the front-line trenches. In effect, he rejected the life that David was leading—enjoying all the comforts of home. Depriving himself of the comforts of home, however, is not the point. "Rather, intercourse would render him ritually unclean for combat" (Halpern 2001, 36). Uriah's sense of propriety and his concern for ritual purity contrast with David's gross impropriety and moral impurity.

Tragically, Bathsheba sat home alone, in the crisis and shame of this unwanted pregnancy. Did she have anyone with whom she could share her anguish? Did she know that Uriah was in town and did not come to her? Would she have told him what David had done? We do not know.

Rather than being put to shame by Uriah's show of honor, David pulled out Plan B from his play book of treachery and put it into action. He had to act quickly if he was going to prevent Uriah from fingering him as the violator of his marriage. He instructed General Joab to put Uriah in the front, where the fighting would be fiercest and then to withdraw so that Uriah would be killed. Uriah would lead the charge while his fellow soldiers would slink away in retreat. So much for being repaid for his loyalty to his king and to his comrades.

Again, David used his royal power not to protect his subjects but to destroy them in order to accomplish his own self-centered ends. When Uriah was dead, the king would marry Bathsheba to cover up the rape and resulting pregnancy. The cover-up came at high cost, but it made for a perfect crime that no one would discover, or so he thought. David had Uriah set up not because he wanted to marry Bathsheba, but because he wanted to conceal the sordid truth behind her unexpected pregnancy. He was consumed by his desire not to lose public face, his legacy—the public persona that he was of upstanding moral character and a worthy king (2 Sam. 8:15). He would do anything to maintain this false face. He was abusing his God-given power so that he could continue to look like a righteous man of God.

David's plan worked to perfection this time; Uriah died in battle a hero. David, who wept over the deaths of his enemies Saul (2 Sam. 1:11–27) and Abner (2 Sam. 3:31–39), shrugs off Uriah's death and the deaths of the others who died with him in following the fateful orders that were a death warrant (2 Sam. 11:14–25). His cold-hearted reaction in 2 Samuel 11:25 may be paraphrased, "Oh well, such is a soldier's sad fate" or "Oh well, we all have to die sometime" (Arnold 2003, 530).

Uriah's death symbolizes what commonly happens when women are abused by men in power. Their husbands also become victims. This abuse kills their marriage, kills them spiritually, and in Uriah's situation, results in physical death. If the violation becomes public, the shame can be so overwhelming that it drives some to suicide or to violent revenge. Uriah never knew the evil done to him by the king he so faithfully served.

The war office notified David of Uriah's death. David told the messenger to tell General Joab words to the effect of, "Don't let this upset you. It's a war after all. Press on." Without remorse, he perceived his reputation to be more important than the life of a faithful servant. He was above it all, above morality, above the law of God. The uniformed soldiers duly notified the new widow that her worst fears had been realized; her husband had fallen in battle. The Bible tells us, "When the wife of Uriah heard that her husband was dead, she made lamentation for him" (2 Sam. 11:26). It is the only mention of emotion in the whole chapter. Bathsheba grieved for what had been stolen from her, the man she had loved. Did David tell her what he had done, pointing out, perhaps, his ability to wield power over life and death, thinking she would be glad to have this opportunity to be his wife? We do not know. But she was not glad over Uriah's death; she grieved. Imagine how her grief would have been compounded had she learned that David had plotted the murder of her husband *because* of her pregnancy. Her inability to protect herself from David had now resulted in her husband's death.

In the Bible, laments call for God to hear, to see, and to intervene. In response to Bathsheba's lament, the Lord does see: "But the thing that David had done was evil in the sight of the LORD" (2 Sam. 11:27, NASB). There is no word here that Bathsheba had done anything to displease the Lord. She is not a coconspirator. This deed was David's. He would not get away with it if God had anything to say about it. And God did!

God Answers Bathsheba's Lament (2 Samuel 12:1–14)

Prophets do not engage in cover-ups, and that is why the true story gets told, though not Bathsheba's side of it. Nathan, like an ancient Detective Columbo, somehow discovered David's evil deeds and was then sent by God to confront the king. He sought to catch David off guard and began by telling him of a horrible crime. It is a parable, but David does not know that until he has fallen into Nathan's trap. It was a brilliant stratagem that exposed the king's guilt. For the first time, David could see in the clear light of God's perspective what he had done and what he had become.

> "There were two men in a certain city, the one rich and the other poor. The rich man had very many flocks and herds; but the poor man had nothing but one little ewe lamb, which he had bought. He brought it up, and it grew up with him and with his children; it used to eat of his

meager fare, and drink from his cup, and lie in his bosom, and it was like a daughter to him. Now there came a traveler to the rich man, and he was loath to take one of his own flock or herd to prepare for the wayfarer who had come to him, but he took the poor man's lamb, and prepared that for the guest who had come to him." Then David's anger was greatly kindled against the man. He said to Nathan, "As the Lord lives, the man who has done this deserves to die; he shall restore the lamb fourfold, because he did this thing, and because he had no pity."

Nathan said to David, "You are the man! Thus says the Lord, the God of Israel: I anointed you king over Israel, and I rescued you from the hand of Saul; I gave you your master's house, and your master's wives into your bosom, and gave you the house of Israel and of Judah; and if that had been too little, I would have added as much more. Why have you despised the word of the Lord, to do what is evil in his sight? You have struck down Uriah the Hittite with the sword, and have taken his wife to be your wife, and have killed him with the sword of the Ammonites. Now therefore the sword shall never depart from your house, for you have despised me, and have taken the wife of Uriah the Hittite to be your wife. Thus says the Lord: I will raise up trouble against you from within your own house; and I will take your wives before your eyes, and give them to your neighbor, and he shall lie with your wives in the sight of this very sun. For you did it secretly; but I will do this thing before all Israel, and before the sun." David said to Nathan, "I have sinned against the Lord." Nathan said to David, "Now the Lord has put away your sin; you shall not die. Nevertheless, because by this deed you have utterly scorned the Lord, the child that is born to you shall die." (2 Sam. 12:2–15)

True to Nathan's word, the Lord struck down the child that Bathsheba bore to David. Sin affects the guilty and the innocent alike. The baby became very ill and died despite David's prayers. And the obituary column recording the names of other beloved children in his family would grow longer.

The story about a sheep was a pinprick in the hot air balloon of David's arrogance and covetousness. There was no hiding the evil now; it was out. The story underscored how precious Bathsheba was to Uriah. Note that in this parable, the little ewe lamb, like Bathsheba, was also a victim. It did not ask to be served up for dinner. Note also that Nathan never confronted Bathsheba or accused her of sin. Nathan said nothing about Bathsheba carrying any responsibility for what had happened; regardless of how she might have felt, she was not to blame.

The story of the lamb does not correspond with what David did at every point, making David's guilt even darker. Unlike the man in the parable of the ewe lamb, David was not offering anyone hospitality, and he took a wife, a human being, not a farm animal loved as a pet. A man with many wives wanted another man's only wife. In the parable, the ewe lamb was slaughtered for dinner, but in the real life story, Uriah was the one slaughtered in battle. Perhaps Bathsheba's soul was also devastated, like unto death. She lost the honorable husband who loved her, her child, her home, and everything about the life she had known, only to be placed in the king's harem. The poor farmer could perhaps be paid four times over for the lamb, but there was no restoring Uriah's life. And we are left uncertain whether Bathsheba's life could ever be restored as well. Even if she could have filed and won a sexual harassment lawsuit, no amount of money in the world would have been enough to undo what had been done to her.

David's violation of Bathsheba did more than destroy her marriage, her child, and life as she had known it, it unleashed a domino effect of evil. David called what he had done sin;

"I have sinned against the Lord," he said to Nathan (2 Sam. 12:13). Nathan, however, called what David had done "evil" (2 Sam. 12:9). It is a subtle but important difference. David discounted the evil he had done by calling it sin. "Sin" implies that abusive behavior is universal, "for all have sinned and fall short of the glory of God" (Rom. 3:23, NIV). We are all sinners, and using the language of sin normalizes and minimizes what David has done. But killing the body and soul of others in order to gratify one's own desires, however, is not universal. Although the potential for what David did may reside in all of us, not all of us are guilty of this kind of evil. Only those with power can do evil of this magnitude. It is this kind of evil that Jesus spoke of when he said that those who caused little ones to stumble might as well have a millstone tied to their necks and be thrown into the sea (Matt. 18:6). For Jesus, causing those who are "little" and who have no power to lose their way is a grave evil worthy of grim punishment, and it can only be committed by those who are the opposite of the "little ones," those who possess power.

It becomes clear that although God could and did forgive David's sin, the evil David had unleashed continued to wreak death and destruction. An innocent baby suffered and died. Bathsheba stood by, again helpless and alone. David's grief was the focus of everyone's attention. Where was Bathsheba—weeping alone?

Where is God's grace for the victim in this story? What was done cannot be undone. Can God create anything good from the shambles David has made of his house, his family? David repents his sin but stays in power. If Psalm 51 is David's confession as it is identified in its heading, "A Psalm of David, when the prophet Nathan came to him, after he had gone in to Bathsheba," his pleas to God for mercy are interesting:

> Have mercy on me, O God,
>> according to your steadfast love;
> according to your abundant mercy
>> blot out my transgressions.

He went on to cry out, "Before you and you alone have I sinned." David still seemed not to understand the enormity of what he had done to others. What about Bathsheba? What about Uriah? But his sin against them *was* his sin against God, and God offers forgiveness to the repentant and humbled David.

One wonders whether Bathsheba ever learned the truth that David had plotted her husband's death, and if so, whether she ever forgave him. If she had not heard it in the rumors flying around the court, perhaps it all came out when Nathan came to call. How did she feel, being seized and brought to the household of the man who had violated her, and then losing the baby that resulted from the rape? David had other wives and children; presumably, this was her first child. The story is about David, however, and so Bathsheba's feelings are never revealed. We are never told how she felt about David or about God. Her silence matches her helplessness. We can only read between the lines to guess what they might have been. The text says that when the baby died, David gives comfort to her (2 Sam. 12:34). His comfort would be laughable if it were not so tragic in its inadequacy. David has not distinguished himself in the accounts of his exploits as a compassionate man. To comfort her, it says, he goes in and lies with her. Whose comfort was this? Nevertheless, God is at work, and Solomon is conceived.

Bathsheba became David's chief royal wife. Solomon eventually became the heir to the throne, though he was not the eldest. He continued the house of David that otherwise would have collapsed, and Bathsheba too received special mention in the genealogy of Jesus (Matt. 1:6), though it was stated so baldly that it would have made David blush and her weep to see it: "David was the father of Solomon, whose mother had been Uriah's wife," the text reads. David was forgiven his sin, but that did not mean forgetting what he had done. Forgiveness does not mean forgetting, pretending not to remember what happened. The text refused to call her "the wife of David." She is recorded in the genealogy of the Messiah, the son of David, as "the wife of Uriah," reminding every reader of the whole story of how David had abused her and killed her husband.

There were complications and plot twists to the very end. Power struggles and court intrigue abound. Abishag took Bathsheba's place as David's young and beautiful concubine and attendant, except that by then, in his old age, David has lost his virility (1 Kings 1:1–4). If Bathsheba felt a twinge of jealousy, she could take comfort that Abishag basically functioned as David's hot water bottle, simply there to warm his bed. The man who could not control his lusts now could not perform sexually. Abishag had access to David, but there was no danger that she would bear a rival heir to the throne.

David's son Adonijah, however, sought to usurp the throne from Solomon. Prompted by the prophet Nathan, Bathsheba took action to protect her son's future. She does not appear in the narrative until David is approaching death. She had become strangely empowered while David had become impotent. She maneuvered to get what the prophet Nathan assured her that God had in store for her son, Solomon.

Her last summons before the king presents a scene different from the first summons. King David commands: "'Summon Bathsheba to me.' So she came into the king's presence, and stood before the king" (1 Kings 1:28). There she insisted that David honor his promise to make Solomon his successor. In the end, Bathsheba as queen mother asserted her power. She had been stripped bare—literally and figuratively—by David. She had experienced a lifetime of grief. Where did the strength and grace to become a survivor come from, especially while living with the very man who had so mistreated her? How do any of us go on when it seems we have lost everything?

First, it is important to look at survival of grief and loss as the task of a lifetime. Overcoming abuse and grief does not happen overnight. Second, God answered her cry of lamentation. When Nathan came to David and told him the terrible parable of the ewe lamb, Bathsheba no longer had to suffer in silence and secrecy. Nathan was her advocate, confronting David openly with the evil he had done to her and to Uriah. Nathan recognized and spoke aloud what David had done. Before Nathan came on the scene, the only person who knew what Bathsheba had suffered was David himself, and he was undoubtedly not a very compassionate support for her. Now Bathsheba could openly grieve her losses. In whom did she confide? David's other wives? The servants? Her mother? We do not know. But the possibility for sharing in her family and community was now possible. Grief and loss carried in secrecy are too heavy for anyone. We need others to hear us when we cry.

Not only did Nathan make the evil done to her public so that she could begin to find her way through it, but he also cleared her of any responsibility for wrongdoing. If she had blamed herself for any of the evil that had befallen her family through David's actions, the prophet Nathan cleared her. It was David. And because of Nathan, David repented.

God answers our prayer in unexpected ways. At the time, it may feel like no answer at all. Bathsheba's lament to God was answered by the prophet Nathan. Because of Nathan, the evil was confronted, David repented, and with God's intervention, Bathsheba and David began a life together that gave Bathsheba purpose as the mother of Solomon, from whose line the Messiah would come.

No one expected her to forget what happened—not even the genealogist of Matthew. She was a woman of sorrows, of losses. We are all quilts of our experiences, sewn together in one fabric of our life. We cannot forget those experiences without forgetting who we are. But she does not deserve the blame and shame that have been visited on her for centuries. Instead, she deserves admiration as a survivor, a woman of strength and purpose.

In the end, it was David who had to consent to her wishes: "As the LORD lives, who has saved my life from every adversity, as I swore to you by the LORD, the God of Israel, 'Your son Solomon shall succeed me as king, and he shall sit on my throne in my place,' so will I do this day" (1 Kings 1:29–30). Bathsheba bowed before her liege and said, "May my lord King David live for ever!" (1 Kings 1:31). But it will not be this King David who lives forever. It will be the Messiah, the Son of God.

No joyful wedding launched Bathsheba and David's family. Instead, they built a family on grief, on loss, on rape, on murder. It makes some of our families' craziness seem tame. Moreover, it was all so public. Gazing from the roof that fateful day upon Bathsheba below, David thought he could sin in private. In the end, everyone in his world both then and since would know what David had done to Bathsheba, and to Uriah, and the reason their infant died. Perhaps because it was public, he could face what he had done and move on. He could not hide from it, from the community, and especially from himself. It is only when we can say, "This is what I have done; this is what suffering I have caused," that we can begin to heal. We find that no sin is too big for God to forgive; no grief is too deep for God to comfort.

7

The Stories of Jephthah's Daughter and David's Daughter Tamar

When Parents Fail

Jephthah and His Daughter (Judges 11)

Jephthah, one of the military commanders who fought off Israel's nemeses during the era of the Book of Judges, gets honorable mention in the Faith Hall of Fame in Hebrews 11:

> And what more should I say? For time would fail me to tell of Gideon, Barak, Samson, Jephthah, of David and Samuel and the prophets—who through faith conquered kingdoms,

administered justice, obtained promises, shut the mouths of lions, quenched raging fire, escaped the edge of the sword, won strength out of weakness, became mighty in war, put foreign armies to flight. (Hebrews 11:32–34)

When one reads the story of Jephthah and his daughter, who is known only as "the daughter of Jephthah the Gileadite," it may give one pause to wonder why he was included in this venerable list. The story has been labeled by one scholar as one of the texts of terror in the Old Testament (Trible 1984). It is not one chosen as a Sunday school lesson for children, and it is hardly apt as a text for a Father's Day sermon, unless the topic is "How to Be a Bad Father." Ending horribly, it seems to have no redeeming value.

Jephthah gets one of the worst introductions in all of scripture: "Now Jephthah the Gileadite, the son of a prostitute, was a mighty warrior. Gilead was the father of Jephthah" (Judg. 11:1). He was one tough customer when it came to making war, but his résumé also notes that he was illegitimate and, worse, the son of a whore, someone who solicited men on the streets. Apparently, his father was a customer, perhaps a regular customer, of the nameless harlot. The fact that a child was conceived from this illicit, commercial union was not about to be kept secret. Word got out that the father of this boy was a gentleman of property, and apparently, Jepthah's mother actually sent him to live with his father, since he had the means to support him. Children belonged to their fathers in that culture. Besides, how could a prostitute provide a proper upbringing for a child? So Jephthah attempted to be a part of his father's family, hanging around in the shadows, always on the fringe of family life. But he was a stain on the family's honor and an embarrassment to the family, and he knew it all too well, since they probably reminded him often of his marginal status. The legitimate sons of Gilead's wife griped, "Who does he think he is? He's not one of us!" We can imagine the pain this little boy suffered, rejected by his brothers, known and called openly "son of a prostitute." His mother had to send him away; his father's family despised him.

As they reached adulthood, the meanness of Jepthah's half-brothers grew uglier. Their bullying and ganging up on him and name calling—"You know what you are? You are a ____"—which tortured him as a child and culminated in their concerted efforts to hound this mongrel out of the family completely. They saw him as a threat to their financial security. Jephthah could potentially drain the family's wealth if he were included in the distribution of their father's inheritance. They schemed together and decided it was in their best interests to get rid of him and drive him as far away from the home-stead as they could. Jephthah is hardly alone in the biblical narrative as a victim of sibling rivalry and the selfish plots of half-brothers. He is also not the first member of a family to be thrown out on his ear. His father is totally silent in the story; we have no idea whether he knew what his sons were doing. If he had cared at all for this son, how could Gilead have allowed him to be taunted all those years? How could his sons force this young man out of his own home and he not know? Gilead does not show much parental affection for Jephthah. Perhaps he intentionally ignored his sons' mean-spirited harassment of their half-brother when they were children and their violent rejection of him when they were adults because it served his purposes. It was a secret relief to him for this unwanted child to be relegated to the shadows and then, as an adult, to just go away. Jephthah had no de-fender, no one who cared for him.

As an outcast, he fled to the land of Tob, where he took up with some ruffians who did not care about someone's past or blemished lineage. He became a raider with this bunch of desperadoes, terrorizing the countryside. One might picture a modern motorcycle gang of Hell's Angels dressed in black leather, wreaking havoc and striking fear among the locals. Jephthah had to learn the art of survival in an unsympathetic and tough world. He had a lot of opportunities to hone his battle skills and tough-guy image. His reputation spread as a valorous, if dangerous, knight errant. Even his half-brothers back home and so far away got wind of his legendary might as a warrior.

Years passed; Jepthah had been gone from home in Gilead for "some time" (Judg. 11:4), and the half-brothers had become "the elders of Gilead" (Judg. 11:5). The Ammonites made war against Israel and were whipping them badly. With their backs to the wall, his half-brothers thought of Jephthah. Hat in hand, they came petitioning the outcast Jephthah to be their military commander for the fight. We wonder why he even allowed them to approach him at all. Perhaps he missed home; they were the only family he had known, and no matter how mean and miserable a family is, we become attached to our families. They tell us who we are and whose we are, even when the message is one of humiliation and rejection. No matter how far we go, we cannot really leave family behind. They travel with us, in the memories and messages they have embedded in our understanding of ourselves.

Jephthah received his half-brothers. Astounded at their request that he risk his life to save them from their enemies, he reminded them that they had hated him openly, rejected him publicly, and violently driven him out of his father's house. They simply mumbled something about letting bygones be bygones: "We are desperate, and we need you back." His only qualification for leadership was that he was a mighty warrior in a band of roughriders, and that was good enough for them. "We will make you our leader if you do this for us." The opportunity to be a respected commander was tantalizing enough, or perhaps that combined with the chance—finally—to be a real member of this family, touched a deep longing in Jephthah. Not only did they promise him a place at the table, they were ready to put him at the *head* of the table. Perhaps he had fantasized since he was a little boy about being needed and wanted by his own family. But even in his childhood dreams, he could have never imagined that he would actually become the head of his father's family. Even though he had serious doubts that God would actually come through and bring victory, he could not say no to the chance that he might finally find himself welcomed at home. We hear the little boy inside this rough warrior, astonished and checking whether they really mean what they say when he replies to them, "Suppose you take me back to fight the Ammonites and the LORD gives them to me—will I really be your head?" (Judg. 11:9) "Really? Do you mean it? You're not lying to me? Honest?" They swear to Jephthah and to the Lord, and so Jephthah agreed to go with them and become their commander-in-chief.

The History of the Parents Visited on the Children (Judges 11:29–33)

Jephthah wasn't sure that God even cared about Israel, let alone this war. The Spirit of the Lord came upon him as he passed through the land recruiting troops for his new army. He felt that God was speaking to him and through him, and that God was going to use him. But how could he be sure? To be doubly sure of victory, he offered God a rash vow: "If you will give the Ammonites into my hand, then whoever comes out of the doors of my house to meet me, when I return victorious from the Ammonites, shall be the Lord's, to be offered up by me as a burnt offering" (Judg. 11:30–31).

What was he thinking? Did he engage his mouth before his brain, and this vow just popped out? What did he think would come out to meet him? A cow or a human? Did he expect to make a human sacrifice? If so, he was trying to pull out all the stops to manipulate God in the same way that Israel's pagan neighbors did with their gods to get their will done. Did he think that as a son of a whore he needed to do something extra to compensate for his lack of a proper pedigree to get God to listen to him? Or, in his insecurity, was he so uncertain about the power of God's Spirit upon him that he thought he could seal the deal by binding God to some bloody contract? So often, God is ready to give us something freely, but we think we need to earn it and try to offer God a trade that God cannot refuse. Jephthah wanted to make sure, to feel like he was in control, rather than to trust God to deliver him and Israel. The results were tragic. He wanted to succeed at all costs and was ready to sacrifice anything if it would help him achieve the desired success. There was nothing in his own household that was as important to him as becoming head of the household of Gilead. He wanted to be known as Israel's deliverer. After being so cruelly rejected, he wanted to rule over others; at long last, they would respect him. He was driven by ambition fueled by childhood abuse that blinded him to God's care and love. He could not see the potential consequences to his nearest and dearest. The job before him came first; he clearly was not thinking about his own family back home in Tob.

The results of the battle exceeded all expectations, however. The victory over the Ammonites was decisive, but victories in life's battles sometimes exact terrible costs. Jephthah's vow must be redeemed (Judg. 11:34–39b). He said "whatever comes out of the doors of my house . . . to meet me" (Judg. 11:31, NIV) he would offer up as a sacrifice. And there she was, his only child, his daughter, the first one to come dashing through the door to greet him. She came running down the lane to throw her arms around her daddy who had come home from the battlefront safe and sound. She came to sing the victory songs of joy with timbrels and dancing, as Miriam did so many years ago (Exod. 15:19–21) and as the women will do when David returns victorious from war (1 Sam. 18:6–7). Jephthah's triumphant swagger was transformed into a stunned, wobbly shuffle when he saw his daughter. She saw the stricken look on her father's face, and her joy quickly evaporated as well, replaced by a rush of uncertain fear. What could possibly be so wrong when everything seemed so right? He was home, safe and victorious. The sound of the tambourines was drowned out by the howls from her father.

Blaming the Victim (Judges 11:34–35)

Jephthah's response to his daughter is a classic case of blaming the victim. He cared only about what this situation meant for himself. He ripped his clothes in a mourning gesture and wailed, "Alas, my daughter! You have brought me very low; you have become the cause of great trouble to me. For I have opened my mouth to the LORD, and I cannot take back my vow" (Judg. 11:35). At the height of his success, he was brought to his knees by his daughter's coming to greet him. She had no idea what he was talking about, but his reproach confirmed that the joyous occasion of his safe return was eclipsed by some terrible unknown trouble that somehow she had caused. Rather than say "I've missed you too" or "It's great to be home again with you," he wailed,

"It's all your fault!" What was her fault? "What have I done now?" she must have wondered. He would break the news to her later. Now he lamented his looming loss as if he were the only one to have to suffer the consequences. He blamed her instead of admitting he had made a faithless, foolish vow. He could have repented and retracted it. But instead, he says, "I cannot take back this vow." How tragic that he did not realize that the God to whom he made this vow abhors human sacrifice. God does not speak one word in this story. Perhaps God is silent because what happened was so unspeakably evil. God abhors the mistreatment of children whom God gives to parents as a special trust. But nowhere does God speak in this text, because Jephthah never asks God, "Is this what you require from me? Is this right? What would you have me do?" Jephthah simply assumes that God is a lot like himself—God works deals, inflicts grief, and authorizes the deaths of innocents.

Jephthah did not offer to die in the place of his daughter. A man of violence is comfortable with violence, even against his only child. He still clung to a false belief that God was as cruel and demanding as he was with his military troops and with his own child. Jephthah could have decided not to fulfill the vow and brought whatever curse God would deliver on his own head. If God were that deficient in compassion, he could take the punishment for a broken vow. It would have saved his daughter's life. Bad theology, bad parenting, and a character warped by the rejection and violence of his own life made for a disastrous combination. He determined to go ahead with sacrificing his daughter instead. It was not God's altar that faced her, but the deadly consequences of her father's own blind ambition. Phyllis Trible writes with some vehemence: "A vow led to victory; victory produced a victim; the victim died by violence; violence has, in turn, fulfilled the vow" (Trible 1984, 104). Both father and daughter are done in by a foolish, faithless vow.

Acceptance of Violence (Judges 11:36–40)

Jephthah's daughter remained unnamed, which was fitting given her lowly heritage. Her grandmother was a harlot, her father was illegitimate, and the story does not even mention her mother. She was alone in the face of her father. She responded with the submissive spirit she had been taught as daughter of this commanding warrior, "Do to me just as you promised" (Judg. 11:36, NIV). She met with courage his cowardly refusal to reconsider his vow. She was ready to give her life without questioning to protect her father's honor and well-being from a God described by her father as one who expected people to keep their promises, even if those promises were to slaughter an innocent child on a fiery altar. She was a trusting child and believed her father, as children do. There was no one to question Jephthah's premise, and so she had no basis to question it herself. She was only a child. She could not think about even appealing to God; why should she? God had been silent when Jephthah had made his rash vow. God had not stopped her from dashing first from the house. No voice boomed now from the heavens to question Jephthah's gloomy pronouncement of her fate. Why would she even think of praying to this God? Children know God from what we teach them. And so she simply replies, "God did his part; I guess you have to do what you have to do" (authors' paraphrase). Her loyalty and complete obedience to her father—"a most welcome characteristic from a patriarchal point of view" (Fuchs 1989, 38)—led to her doom.

She did make one last request. "Let me wander the hills with my girlfriends for two months and bewail my virginity" (authors' paraphrase). If bearing children was everything, as she believed, her life would never be fulfilled. There would be no heir to remember her. Her father had been driven to the hills earlier in his life, and she now took to the hills to lament her evil fate.

After two months, she would come back as promised, and Jephthah would follow through on his vow. For two months, he had time to reconsider. Even if in the first moments of his return he saw no alternative, surely in two months he had time to think it over. But he considered no other way. He is not some heartless villain, but someone who "is shown as a helpless victim of unforeseen circumstances, caught in the web of conflicting allegiances, and insurmountable restraints" (Fuchs 1989, 39). Jephthah had allowed the circumstances of his own life to harden his heart beyond any hope of saving his daughter's life. Perhaps he was enjoying the heady new opportunity to command all of Israel after being an outcast for so many years. She was gone to the hills, and he could simply focus on his victory, not on what he was willing to pay for it. After all, he blamed her; if she had just stayed in the house where she belonged, this would not have happened. The terrible reality of blaming others for our own sins is that we fail to see that we can repent, we can change, we can sometimes give our stories and the stories of those we love a different ending. But taking responsibility for our sins costs us our pride; we have to admit our wrongdoing. Jephthah's pride was too hard-won. He would not give it up.

We are spared the gruesome details of Jephthah's execution of his own daughter. No angel yelled, "Stop!" Heaven did not thunder. No ram was caught in the thicket to serve as a substitute. God had not ordered this execution, and so God does not intervene. One would have thought that human sacrifice would have forever been abandoned in Israel since the time God tested Abraham to see if Abraham would sacrifice his son. Alas, the message had not reached Jephthah. The king of Moab offered up his son, the one who would succeed him, as a burnt offering on the wall when the battle was going against him (2 Kings 3:21–27). Such was not to be done among the people of God, however. Moses warned Israel to take care that they did not do as the people around them did. Israelites were not to say about their pagan neighbors, "I wonder if what they do for their gods might work for us." Pagans committed every imaginable abomination; "they would even burn their sons and their daughters in the fire to their gods." And God hated it. It stank to heaven (Deut. 12:30–31). Human sacrifice was no sacrifice; it was simply murder. Jephthah's was an inhuman human sacrifice of a child by a father too insecure to trust in a gracious God, too full of pride to reconsider his vow, and too concerned with his own life to protect the life of his child. He goes down in history as a terrifying figure, little different from the pagan king of Moab.

Many Christians and Jews cringe over this barbarity and seek to argue that Jephthah did not kill his daughter as a burnt offering. One advantage of being female was that females were not acceptable as sacrifices. She could not be offered on the altar, they suggest, but she could be dedicated to God as Samuel was by his mother, Hannah (1 Sam. 1:27–28). They argue that she was consigned to life as a virgin and consequently destined to be one of the unremembered. If so, we might be able to breathe a sigh of relief, but this seems to be only wishful thinking. The term used here always refers to an actual sacrifice that is burnt upon an altar; it is not used in a figurative sense (see, for example, Gen. 22:2 and 2 Kings 3:27). Walter Sundberg cites an unpublished lecture by Dianne Jacobsen: "Israel looked unflinchingly at the dark side of human ambition and power. Judges exemplifies one of the chief wonders of the Old Testament: namely, its ability to tell the story of Israel critically and candidly. This remarkable people of the ancient past knew how to face up to the sinful consequences of self-absorption" (Sundberg 1993, 87).

A similar story is told about Saul, but with a different ending. When Saul in the heat of battle against the Philistines "laid an oath on the troops, saying, 'Cursed be anyone who eats food before it is evening and I have been avenged on my enemies,'" it is labeled by the narrator as "a very rash act" (1 Sam. 14:24). His son Jonathan did not get word of the prohibition and ate some honey from a honeycomb. Saul found out and this conversation between father and son is recorded (1 Sam. 14:43–44):

Saul:	"Tell me what you have done."
Jonathan:	"I tasted a little honey with the tip of the staff that was in my hand; here I am, I will die."
Saul:	"God do so to me and more also; you shall surely die, Jonathan!"

It looked like another child would bite the dust, but the people rose up in protest and ransomed him from this fate (1 Sam. 14:45–46). In the moral twilight zone, which marked the days of the Judges, no one stepped up to stop Jephthah from following through on his rash vow.

Like so many children of thoughtless, ruthless fathers, the daughter was sacrificed. Jephthah got his wish to become the ruler in Israel. Amazingly, he is not remembered in the New Testament for his faithless, ruthless vow, for his terrifying portrayal of God, for blaming his daughter for what was his own failing, and for his cowardly murder of his own child to protect himself from whatever punishment he imagined a vengeful God might visit on him. He is counted among the faithful, but he is grouped together with others who had feet of clay—Gideon, Barak, Samson, and David (Heb. 11:32). They had rescued Israel out of the hands of her enemies on every side, according to 1 Samuel 12:11, but in Jephthah's case, he needed rescuing from himself.

Remembering

What is extraordinary to the narrator is that a woman whom we would expect to have died as one of the unremembered—she died childless, having never known a man—was indeed remembered. She suffered horrific injustice, but she was not completely blotted out from all memory. Though her name was lost to history, the daughters of Israel chanted dirges to remember what was done to her. We remember her not as we do her father, but for her courage, for her willingness to die in the belief that in doing so, her father could live blameless before God, having fulfilled his vow. She gave her life for his success in battle. Jephthah suffered for the sins of his parent. But his child bore the ultimate suffering. The unfaithfulness of her grandparents reached to this third generation to bear despicable fruit (Trible 1981). Jephthah's daughter could have run away in order to live. Tragically—and faithfully—she returns to her father at the end of the two months. And he kills her. The rejection of the little boy by mean-spirited brothers inflamed a lifetime of violence and warring, blowing up into the ultimate rejection of his daughter.

Jephthah went on with his life. He led the armies of Israel for another six years after his daughter's death, in a career of violence against his neighbors until his own death (Judges 12). We do not kill our children on altars today, but many of us do sacrifice them on the altars of the relentless pursuit of worldly success. Sundberg draws a parallel to our contemporary situation: "Do not we live in a time of chaos without fixed rules and order? Have we not embraced a Dionysian excess in which self-exaltation has become a dominant criterion for living? Has not the family suffered because mothers and fathers give themselves over to careers and passions? Jephthah's public victory cost him tragic defeat in his private life. Do we not, in our day, repeat both his triumph and anguish?" (Sundberg 1993, 87). Who in our families pays for our ambition?

The Rape of Tamar by Her Brother (2 Samuel 13)

Jephthah's daughter was not the last child to suffer terribly at the hands of a father who misused his power. In the story of David's daughter, Tamar, who was raped by her brother, David does not use his power at all. He passively allows his firstborn son, Amnon, to run amok. All he does is shake his head in dismay while Tamar is inconsolable over her bitter humiliation at the hands of her brother. The unraveling of his family was prophesied by the prophet Nathan when he confronted the king for misusing his power in raping Bathsheba and having her husband, Uriah, killed to cover it up. God was not silent, sending the prophet Nathan to predict doom and family heartache (1 Sam. 12:10–12). The result of the breakdown of morals in David's life was the breakup of his family. It is not that God deliberately wreaked havoc in David's family life; it was the outworking of David's own sin. He committed unspeakable acts, and God simply allowed the consequences of those actions to work themselves out in his life.

David's rash private acts perpetrated in secret and covered up, Nathan says, would have public, family consequences, just as Jephthah's rashly and quietly breathed vow to God became the very public end to his family that was lamented across the hills of his homeland. David, also a violent man, would be plagued by a cycle of violence in his own family. David, a lustful man, would be bedeviled by the sexual violence of his own son. His firstborn son, Amnon, would rape his half-sister Tamar. Once, David may have been proud of him as a chip off the old block, and, alas, he was. He somehow learned from his father to abuse women. Tamar's brother Absalom, whom David loved, would kill Amnon in retaliation for what Amnon did to Tamar. He would then lead a rebellion that would force David to abandon Jerusalem and run for his life. Absalom would then rape ten of David's concubines in broad daylight on the roof—presumably the same roof where David first spied on Bathsheba. Had he not come to a bloody end at the hands of David's general, Joab, he would have forced David from the throne.

Unlike the courage and sacrifice that characterized Jephthah's daughter, David's sons committed the same kinds of wicked deeds that peppered David's career as warrior and king. The sins of the father were played out in the lives of his children, while David watched in horror. It was almost as if watching his children's sin and destruction was part of his punishment for his own sins. David's sin lived on in the family, its scarlet thread tripping one member after another. Most families would desperately fight to keep such an unseemly story about incestuous rape secret, but this torrid tale of rape and murder is reported in the Bible for generations to read. As God promised (2 Sam. 12:12), everything would come to light.

Unchecked Lust (2 Samuel 13:1–14)

The episode begins by noting that David's daughter Tamar was beautiful (2 Sam. 13:1), perhaps too beautiful for her own good. She possessed the kind of beauty that makes a father a little nervous when the boys start to hang around. Fathers never trust the good intentions of the boys who eagerly line up to date their beautiful daughters, perhaps remembering their own intentions when they were young. But a father would hardly suspect his own son of having designs on his sister. It was a complex family of multiple wives and half-siblings, to be sure, but a family nevertheless. The text emphasizes that Amnon and Tamar were indeed brother and sister, which serves to underscore the heinous nature of the sin (2 Sam. 13:11–12; 20). The word *brother* occurs ten times, *sister* eight times, *son* three times, and *father* once in this story. That last statistic may be part of the problem; the father is mostly absent. David did nothing as a father to discipline his son, protect his daughter, or console her in her grief.

Amnon became "lovesick" over Tamar. It was not really love. He had fallen in hormone-driven lust, but he called it love. True love begins when someone else's needs are more important than one's own. William Blake captured it in a poem from his *Songs of Experience*, "The Clod and the Pebble:"

> Stanza 1
> Love seeketh not itself to please
> Nor for itself hath any care
> But for another gives its ease
> And builds a Heaven in Hell's despair
> ....
> Stanza 3
> Love seeketh only Self to please
> To bind another to its delight
> Joys in another's loss of ease
> And builds a Hell in Heaven's despite

Amnon's love was only erotic attraction, a vacuum in his soul craving to be filled. It is the kind of passion from which no one is safe. It can thrust one from the heights of bliss down to the abyss of misery, and in the process it mauls those victims who might get in its sights.

Amnon was bedeviled by this frightful, hormone-driven lust. Not only was his sister in danger, but he was about to begin a cycle of destruction that would cost him his life and nearly cost David his throne. He was consumed with gnawing sexual desire for Tamar. He allowed himself to spend his days in moping obsession, so much so that his friend Jonadab asked him, "What's gotten into you? You are always mooning about." He answered, "Tamar! I am smitten. I love her with all my heart, but she hardly gives me the time of day."

To help his poor, lovesick friend, Jonadab hatched a plot by which Amnon could gaze more fully on her beauty. "Why don't you feign being sick. Go to bed. When your dad comes around to see how you're doing, tell him you need someone you can trust to prepare the food to help you recover. You never know. Somebody might be trying to poison you as the heir to the throne. Then tell him to send Tamar to fix you some wholesome bread where you can watch her. We will think up something to empty out the house, and when she shows up, you've got her."

Jonadab was some friend, feeding Amnon a scheme to do violence to his own sister. Amnon's rape of his sister would be no careless, impulsive act. He carefully plotted, taking to his bed to play the sick invalid while waiting to snare his sister.

David doted on his firstborn son and was duly worried about his sudden illness.

"Are you going to be all right?" David asked,

"Yeah, Dad, but can you get Tamar to fix me something to eat to help get back on my feet?"

The unsuspecting David said, "Okay, I will tell Tamar to fix you something nice to help you get well. She will do as I say."

Tamar came to her brother like a ministering angel. She may have wondered why her brother always seemed to look at her in that way that made her self-conscious and uncomfortable. She could not quite put her finger on it, though. Now he was sick, and her father, the king, had told her to cook for his heir to the throne. She could not refuse her father, no matter how uncomfortable Amnon made her feel. By the order of her father, she went to Amnon's house and made and baked bread for Amnon while he watched her from his bed. He refused to get up and come eat, however, instead ordering everyone out of the house so that they would be alone. Like the wolf in the Little Red Riding Hood story, he wanted her to get closer so he could grab her and she could not escape. "Bring it into the bedroom and please feed it to me," he said in a pitiful, weak voice intended to evoke her sympathy. When she came close, he leapt from the bed and seized her roughly. Then, in a flash of horror, Tamar knew that it was all a plot. She knew what he wanted. She tried to reason with him and buy some time. She screamed, "No! This kind of thing is not done in Israel! Please do not disgrace me. You will ruin us both. If you want me so badly, just ask the king, our Father, to give me to you in marriage. He will never deny you. You know that. He has always given you anything you asked for. He will let us marry. Please do not do this to me!"

She tried to argue that if he did this thing he would not be regarded as a prince of Israel but as a fool, and she was right. He would go down in history as worse than a fool, as an incestuous rapist. She may have been trying to stall him just to try to escape; she was definitely trying to protect herself from him.

But her youthful wisdom goes unheeded; aflame with lust, Amnon would not listen to reason. He wanted one thing, and he was going to get it, and he did not care that it was a crime against her spirit, soul, and body, and against his own as well. The setup was terribly perfect. No one was around to hear her screams or come to her rescue. He had seen to that. He overpowered her and raped her. Rape is rooted in violence and hatred, and from what happened next, it was clear that he felt no love for her. When he was through, he looked at her with cold disinterest and told her to get lost. He treated her as though she were a cheap slut, and now that was exactly how he saw her. He had never seen her as a person to be loved but as a body to be used for his own desires. He got what he wanted and was ready to throw her away and move on to other conquests.

Rejection and Wretchedness (2 Samuel 13:15–22)

The rape obliterated Tamar's personhood. Her clothes were rent asunder; her life was rent asunder. Would anyone listen to her and believe her? How could she put words to what had just happened to her? How could she speak of it? Could she ever tell her father? He would never believe that Amnon could do such a thing. Even if he did, he might buy Amnon's excuse that she was asking for it. She could not speak about it, but she had to say something. She did the only thing she knew to do to blow the whistle on her brother, David's beloved firstborn. She walked around the palace grounds with ashes on her head as a token of her desolation, weeping and wailing. She ripped the costly embroidered robe she was wearing, rending the sign of her status as the virgin princess. The word for this robe is used elsewhere only in Genesis 37:3 for the coat of many colors that Jacob gave to his son Joseph because he loved him more than any of his other children. The robe may have been given to her by David. He may not have showered her with love and attention, but he gave her gifts instead. Ripping this garment proclaimed loudly and clearly that her status as a marriageable virgin and her future prospects had been shredded. How long did she bewail her condition and dissolve in tears before someone asked her what was wrong?

Tamar may have asked herself, "What did I do wrong that God allowed this to happen to me? Was I not good? Was I not good enough? Did I somehow deserve this?" Barbara Brown Taylor gives a simple answer to such questions: "Goodness is no protection from pain." She goes on to say:

> If life teaches us that core truth, our faith confirms it. Jesus was as good as good gets, and still he suffered pain—all kinds of pain—not only physical pain but also spiritual and emotional pain. By facing into it instead of running away from it, he showed us a new way to live, but few of us have followed. In spite of everything he said and did, most of us still cling to our own version of the truth: namely, that if we are very, very good, God won't let anything bad happen to us. We will be protected. We will be spared. It is a great perversion of the gospel, but it is also very human. (Taylor 1998, 57–58)

During Tamar's pain, David, her father, proved to be both blind and naive and offered her no consolation. He had unwittingly abetted the crime by ordering Tamar to go to her brother. When word of the transgression reached his ears, he was furious, but then he did nothing. Was it because he thought, "What's done is done"? Or did he identify all too well with his son? He knew how lust, if fed, could lead one to plot and carry out terrible acts that one would regret later. Did he just say to himself in resignation, "What are you going to do?" He loved Amnon; he did not want to destroy his relationship with his son. He would just ignore it. That appears to be one of his problems as a parent. According to 1 Kings 1:6, David never confronted his son Adonijah either when he needed correction. It says that "never at any time" did he displease his son by asking, "Why have you done thus and so?" So, the boys in David's family were used to getting away with murder, so to speak. He was also used to treating women as insignificant objects and maybe thought that his daughter would just have to get over it. It is interesting that he had visited his sick son, but the text says nothing about him visiting his devastated daughter after she was violated. She was left bereft and inconsolable. He appeared not to notice that she would break into sobs and walk around the palace with ripped clothes and ashes on her head. Maybe he thought, "She is just going through one of those stages. Who understands women?"

What is clear is that Amnon would have nothing to do with Tamar. She had served his purposes. Now, as far as he was concerned, she was just trash he put out in the street for the garbage collectors to pick up and haul away. This reveals him to be a classic abuser. He says things that are cruel, hurtful, and degrading. He curses at her and threatens even worse violence. In public, people think he is jovial, friendly, and the life of the party. Few know that he is a Dr. Jekyll and Mr. Hyde, and they never see his private transformation into a violent rapist. Certainly, his father could not accept it and would have believed his pathological lies to cover up what he did and to put all the blame on his Siren sister.

It seems that David either did not care about his daughter or did not know how to express his care. She wanted her daddy and longed to be held and comforted in his arms. But he may have wanted her to keep silent so that it would all go away, and he lent support to his son's evil ways with a callous disregard for what he had done. No use crying over spilt milk, or, in this case, the spilt blood of a virgin daughter. David attempted to keep peace at any price, including ignoring his daughter so that he could maintain his relationship with this soulless, abusive son whose path would bring them destruction.

Unchecked Revenge (2 Samuel 13:23–39)

Tamar's full brother Absalom did notice her weeping, and he did care. "Do you mean our father hasn't done anything about this?" he asked. "He hasn't lifted a finger against that slimy worm Amnon? It is all because he is the firstborn and the heir," he fumed. "We'll see about that!" When they passed each other in the hallways, one can imagine that Absalom looked daggers at Amnon. He would not speak a word to him and was biding his time, nursing the rage silently in his heart just as Amnon had nursed his lust for his sister. Absalom urged his sister not to take what had happened to heart, to be quiet—for now. He had no intention of putting this wrong behind him, however, but instead fed the growing hatred for his brother. His anger festered like a splinter deep in his soul, poisoning everything with an obsession for revenge. Anger is a warning that there is trouble in a relationship; when the trouble is not addressed, simple rage becomes despising hatred. The other becomes not a person with whom one has a terrible problem, but instead a dehumanized target to be hit and destroyed. The focus becomes vindication of self and revenge, not restoration of a broken relationship.

One can only imagine the tension in this royal household. In her desolation, Tamar retreated into hiding in the household of Absalom. The hatred between the brothers was palpable. And the king, though furious, simply overlooked it all, hoping against hope that this latest travesty would somehow just fade from everyone's memory. There was no chance of that, however.

Two years later, Absalom threw a party for the sheepshearing time, out in the country, near the border, and invited the whole family. David begged off. He said it was a great idea, but he could not come. He was getting on in years, and perhaps he preferred to stay home. He gave the excuse that the whole family would surely be a burden in the middle of this busy season of work. "Well, be sure to send Amnon and the other brothers!" Absalom demanded. "We are going to have a great time." David may have been a little worried about this suggestion, but surely Absalom did not still bear a grudge over that incident with Tamar. No one had said anything, after all. David mistook family quiet for family peace. David ordered Amnon to go to the party as he had ordered his daughter Tamar to go to Amnon. Again, it was a fateful order, one that could not be refused.

Like Dinah's brothers years before, Absalom decided to take vengeance into his own hands for the rape of his sister, since it appeared that his father had done absolutely nothing to seek justice for his daughter, much less to make Amnon responsible for his despicable self-gratifying violence. Absalom and his buddies would have Amnon just where they wanted him, unprotected, and off guard in a partying mood. They would ply him with hooch until he was drunk, and then Absalom would give the orders for his men to attack. "Kill him! Don't worry about the king," he assured them. "I will soon be the one giving the orders around here." It was like a scene from some Mafia movie. When the time came, the thugs struck, and Amnon lay dead in a pool of his own blood.

The other brothers flew out of there as fast as their mules could run, racing toward home in a cloud of dust, believing that Absalom was planning to have them murdered as well.

Violent abuse, deceit, and false quiet had created a family in which anything could happen. In the hubbub, the rumor reached the palace that Absalom had killed all of the sons of David. Now, David lamented. He ripped his clothes as Tamar had ripped hers, and he threw himself down to the floor sobbing as Tamar had sobbed. Nathan's prophecy may have flashed across his mind. It was all coming true. It was all coming to this. Jonadab raced in to say that it was not as bad as all that. They only got Amnon; the rest got away. Only Amnon died. David did not see it that way. He did not breathe a sigh of relief but lamented the loss of his son, a grief that would mark the rest of his life. Actually, he lost two sons that day, and he had lost a daughter two years before, and his love child with Bathsheba even before that—all lost to him because of the sin he had unleashed in his own family. Absalom absconded to the same hills where his father used to hide out when he was being hunted by King Saul. He roamed there for three years, ignoring his father's pleas to come home. He would eventually come back, but it would be in full revolt in an attempt to usurp his father's throne, starting a civil war that would rip apart the nation.

Grief upon Grief (2 Samuel 18:33)

Absalom's revolt almost succeeded, but it ultimately fell short, and all of the conspirators were killed. Absalom fled for his life, with David pleading with General Joab to spare his life if they ever caught him. Joab disobeyed the order, killing Absalom with his own hands when he got his hair caught in the branches of a low-hanging oak tree while trying to flee on a mule. With Absalom's arms flailing about helplessly, Joab drove him through with a spear. Joab probably could not understand King David's love for his son after all the heartache he caused him. David, he thought, did not know his own best interests, and so he took matters into his own hands and eliminated Absalom and any possibility of another rebellion. Joab then had his body thrown into a pit, and when the news reached David, he wept uncontrollably. He cried out, "O my son Absalom! My son, my son Absalom! If only I had died instead of you—O Absalom, my son, my son!" (2 Sam. 18:33, NIV). David grieved over the loss of his sons (2 Sam. 13:39; 2 Sam. 18:33–19:5). He had other sons and other daughters, but it did not assuage the pain of his loss. As Marcia Falk says, "More doesn't help, doesn't matter. I don't have two children: I have two ones, two onlys. Human relationships do not fill in for, do not substitute for, do not replace each other" (Falk 1994, 63). But it is sad to note that the narrator records no tears shed by David over what happened to his daughter. What happened to her was like death, but apparently his grief over what happened to her was more constrained.

This sordid affair has a direct effect on who will succeed David as king. Amnon, first in line, was killed by Absalom in revenge. Now Absalom was dead. Who would become the heir? Ironically, it would be Solomon, the son of the woman he himself had raped and whose husband he had murdered.

Family Failure; God's Redemption

Where was Tamar during all this murder, intrigue, and insurrection? We do not know. She is well offstage. We know only that Absalom married and had three sons, who go unnamed, and a daughter he named Tamar in honor of his sister (2 Sam. 14:27). She too was a beautiful woman. But is this all that life holds for Tamar as a consequence of her brother's violence?

The stories of sexual violence and murder in the Bible reveal the depths of human depravity and hit us with a recognition of our own sinfulness, although ours seems domesticated when compared with the fiery human sacrifice, false pride, violent incest, murder, and insurrection of these families. Even so, when we read about Jephthah blaming his daughter for the consequences of his own faithless vow, we realize that we too have a tendency to blame others instead of taking responsibility for our failures and sins. When we allow childhood hurts to shape our adult character, the way Jephthah did, and then wreak havoc on those we say we love the most, we see ourselves even in the terrible figure of Father Jephthah. When we allow selfish desires to become obsessions that turn others into objects to be discarded like a paper cup drained of its contents, we are like the lustful Amnon. When we lie to ourselves and say that the quiet that covers pain in our families is peace, we allow hurt to fester into family boils that poison the family blood, like Father David did. When we nurse anger into revenge-seeking rage that seeks destruction rather than healing, though perhaps with stabbing words that mean to wound rather than with the spear Absalom used to kill his brother, we echo into our own families the sin of Absalom.

Where is the hope? How can God possibly bring any good from all this family failure? Somehow, God traced through these ugly stories a trail of promise, of love, of redemption. One who will be known as the Son of David, who will suffer on a cross, a hideous and vicious torture invented by hideous and vicious minds, will reveal the plan that was there all along. Nothing we can do can separate us from God's love—not a broken vow, or a parent's rejection, or a violent rape, or even murdering our own family members, whether with swords or with words meant to destroy the very self. God promises to forgive us and restore our brokenness. If God forgives us, then surely, we can admit our failures to one another and ask for forgiveness and restoration. We can start over together. We are being redeemed, day by day.

A motif in the Book of Judges is expressed by the statement: "In those days there was no king in Israel; all the people did what was right in their own eyes" (Judg. 17:6; 21:25). The story of Jephthah reveals that he was no different from anyone else in that era. But there could have been a different end to this story. No one emerges from a troubled family history and social ostracism without scars. The taunt, "You are a bastard who will never amount to anything," may have played over and over again in the back of his mind, but Jephthah could have transformed the pain of childhood rejection into joy that would have not have brought ruination to his own daughter. He was resilient, not helpless and vulnerable. Plus, if he had fully realized it, the Spirit of the Lord was upon him. He did not need to resort to a vow to help win a battle and win acceptance by his kindred. They treated him shabbily, but he had overcome that. They needed him as much as he needed their approval. Had he known God's grace that accepted him as he was regardless of his heritage, he could have passed it on to his daughter.

The story of David reveals that having a king did not do much to improve the moral climate from the days of the judges. It would take a different kind of king and a different son of David to bring about any real change. This son of David would prohibit all oaths and vows (Matt. 5:33–37), reject unrestricted blood vengeance (Matt. 5:38–42), and warn against nursing anger and lust in the heart (Matt. 5:21–30). He would comfort the oppressed and lift up the downtrodden.

Jephthah and David appear in the showcase of biblical luminaries in Hebrews 11 with many other heavy hitters on the list. If one looks more carefully at their lives, however, each one of them had his or her own faults, blindspots, and problems. Even though they are in the Bible, they were not much different from us. God was not limited by their limitations.

8

The Ethiopian Eunuch

God's Message of Good News

Acts 8:26–40

From Jephthah and David we take the huge leap now to the New Testament and teachings of Jesus about family. Jesus's own family provided the context for much of Jesus's teaching about family. Early in Jesus's ministry, his mother, Mary, and his brothers attempted to rein him in and protect him from the brewing hostilities toward him. Mary went with them to fetch him home. It was not a friendly visit; they wanted to "take charge of him." The same verb is used elsewhere in Mark (6:17; 12:12; 14:1, 44, 46, 49, 51) to mean "to seize forcibly." If he would just lie low for awhile, she may have thought, some of the ruckus and the possible dishonor he was bringing to the family would die down. When she and the brothers arrived where he was teaching, they could not get in the door, so she sent word through the crowd that she was outside asking for him. Jesus ignored her message and used his family's presence as an opportunity to revolutionize the definition of family:

> And he replied, "Who are my mother and my brothers?" And looking at those who sat around him, he said, "Here are my mother and my brothers! Whoever does the will of God is my brother and sister and mother." (Mark 3:33–35)

Jesus no longer restricted the definition of family to biological kinship or legal relationships. Family is composed of those who join themselves in obedience to God and, consequently, to others who have chosen to follow Jesus. Jesus's response to the visit from his family was shocking. It ran counter to cultural wisdom and social expectations. Family was the source of a person's very identity and certainly of social and economic security. In the first-century Mediterranean world, others knew a person as a member of a group or family: there was no such concept as "individualization" or even personal identity (Garland 1996, 131).

The genealogies and laws relating to family life in the scriptures highlight family or clan (and village) membership. The Old Testament uses *life* almost interchangeably with *family*. To reject family or to be cast out of the family meant losing one's life (see Luke 14:26). The purpose of family was to preserve its blood relationships, its wealth, and its honor (see Sirach 26:19–21). When Jesus moved the definition of family away from these blood relationships, he threatened the whole socioeconomic order. Now, according to Jesus, God alone, who is the head of a new divine family, deserves ultimate devotion. Membership in this family is open to all persons regardless of race, class, or gender. The only requirement is that they share Jesus's commitment to God (see Garland 1996, 131).

Bo Prosser shares his experience of the church modeling this kind of family in his own life:

> When my dad divorced my mother, I felt that he also divorced me. He wanted out of our family. When our broken family was trying to make sense of it all, several key families from my home church adopted me. They let me be a part of their families. They loved me unconditionally, fed me unselfishly, and tolerated me lovingly. How thankful I am for Bill and Ruby and Bundy and Anna, for Marion and Linda and their girls! These folks modeled family in the most healthy, intimate, and spiritual ways. They modeled what it meant to do the will of the Father, what it meant to be in the family of Jesus. (Prosser 2006, 63)

Jesus's teaching about families is good news when biological families fail us—as they always will, since they are formed by the kinds of broken people whose lives we have been exploring in earlier chapters. At the same time, Jesus's teaching about family contributed ultimately to the decision of the religious leaders of the day that he deserved death; his redefinition of family undermined the very social order.

The Gospel of John records the last teaching of Jesus about family before his death. Mary was standing at the foot of the cross with the beloved disciple beside her. We can only imagine the agony she was experiencing, to stand helplessly by while her son was tortured. Straining to have breath to speak, Jesus uttered words that sound like a wedding ceremony, when new families are birthed. This was a very different kind of wedding, however. Looking at his mother and referring to his friend standing next to her, Jesus said, "Woman, here is your son." Then looking at the disciple, he made the binding words mutual: "Here is your mother." The very next verse states that Jesus knew that "all was now finished" (John 19:26–28). Proclaiming this new family was a crowning stroke in his earthly ministry.

Family was no longer a way of tracing bloodlines but of tracing faith lines. This family's wealth consisted not of protecting and increasing money and land to pass from one generation to the next but of sharing in common with those in need. Moreover, this was real family, not just the use of terms like "family of God," or calling one another "brother" or "sister" at church because we cannot remember one another's names. "From that time on," John 19:27 says, the beloved disciple took Mary into his own home. He was a real son to her.

If Jesus had not spoken them into existence as an adoptive family, would they have cared for one another in this way? Perhaps, but clearly, naming the relationship had power. Perhaps Jesus could have spoken to the group in a way we might have expected: "You take care of one another when I'm gone." But he was not telling the church to be a caring community; he was turning people *within* the community into an adoptive family. Naming the relationship "family" strengthens and transforms the tie (Garland 2003).

After Jesus's death, the first church in Jerusalem grew rapidly into a large, close community. They shared meals and distributed material resources to the needy among them. A number of Galileans had taken up residence in the city, and a common fund was necessary to support all the members of the fellowship. Former fishermen could not earn much in a place like Jerusalem. Their community inspired by the Spirit was contagious; every day, new people joined them (Acts 2:44–47). They had become, as Jesus promised, one big extended family: "Truly I tell you, there is no one who has left house or wife or brothers or parents or children, for the sake of the kingdom of God, who will not get back very much more in this age, and in the age to come eternal life" (Luke 18:29–30). The Holy Spirit had knit Jesus's followers into a family that transcended the kinship bonds of flesh and blood.

In Forrest Carter's account of Depression-era life in the 1930s, the grandfather explains to his grandson his use of the phrase, "I kin you." It meant to love and to understand.

> Granpa said back before his time "kinfolks" meant any folks that you understood and had an understanding with, so it meant "loved folks." But people got selfish, and brought it down to mean just blood relatives; but that actually it was never meant to mean that. (Carter 1976, 38)

Like all families, this new family had its problems, however. As the family grew, it did not take long for the human side of their life together to poke through the appearance of harmony, and grumbling and discontent began to surface. It was usually styles of life, not simply ideas, that caused the divisions among Jews. The new Christian body joined Jewish-living Jewish Christians and Greek-living Jewish Christians, and the mix of different cultures created problems. These people had seen tongues as of fire resting on one another's heads when the Spirit first came upon them (Acts 2:1–4) and had witnessed miraculous healings in their daily life together. Yet they began to complain about how their leaders were running the church. The daily life of family inevitably brings conflict, even in the holiest of folks.

The first issue to come out into the open sounds like a typical church family or stepfamily squabble. Transplants from foreign lands shaped by the Greek culture of their upbringing fussed that the Hebrews were taking better care of the Hebrew widows than they were the Greek widows. Greek widows, they claimed, were not getting as much food in the daily distribution (Acts 6:1). One can almost hear brothers and sisters at the dinner table: "Mom, his piece of cake is bigger than mine! That's not fair!"

Many Jews in the Diaspora came back to Jerusalem to live out their old age. When men died, they left widows with no relatives to support them. These Christian women had no one and looked to the church to be their family, as Jesus had promised. When death or family dismemberment leaves us alone, when our blood relatives are not there for us for whatever the reason, Christians still have family, the family that Jesus envisioned would be stronger than ties of blood. The widows in this family of Christ were to be cared for, and the early Christians sought to fulfill their obligations to them. To invite all to share in meals fulfilled Jesus's exhortation, "But when you give a banquet, invite the poor, the crippled, the lame, and the blind. And you will be blessed, because they cannot repay you, for you will be repaid at the resurrection of the righteous" (Luke 14:13–14).

After his resurrection, when Jesus was eating with his disciples again, he said in his last conversation with Peter, "Simon son of John, do you love me more than these? . . . Feed my lambs. . . . Simon son of John, do you love me? . . . Tend my sheep. . . . Simon son of John, do you love me? . . . Feed my sheep" (John 21:15–17). Taking care of the lambs also means feeding them literally, and it is a way to show our love of Jesus. While Jewish communities typically cared for the needy with first-century versions of soup kitchens and charity funds, when Christians shared food together, it took on added significance, because eating together was regarded as communion with Christ. The breaking of bread could only remind them of what Jesus had done at his last supper with his disciples and reminded them also of the redeeming significance of his broken body and death (Matt. 22:26–29). The disciples on the road to Emmaus had their eyes opened so that they could recognize the resurrected Jesus only after he broke bread with them and blessed it (Luke 24:13–35).

The task of feeding the sheep in the early community provoked squabbling. It was not just about equitable food distribution. The root problem concerned how very different people could be bound into a family so that no one would feel left out. This Christian family must deal with dynamics much like that of blending two family cultures into a stepfamily. We do not shortchange our own mothers, but these Greek widows apparently were not yet viewed as "our mothers"—and that was the challenge. The basic daily acts of feeding one another and eating together often are the staging ground for these challenges. A stepmother told of cleaning off the table after breakfast. Seeing a half glass of milk left in her daughter's glass, she drank it. She then poured the milk left in her stepdaughter's glass in the cat's dish. Only family members eat and drink from the same dishes. Becoming family does not take place at a moment in time, like a thunderbolt. It is rather a process of imperfect people learning to love one another. Perhaps no family models the teaching of Jesus more than the blending of two broken families into one, whether it is single parents uniting their families in a stepfamily or a family adopting a foster child. It is hard work, but it is the work to which Jesus called us.

The twelve apostles found food distribution and the petty bickering to be a distraction from what they regarded to be the vital ministry of the word. They said, "It is not right that we should neglect the word of God in order to wait at tables" (Acts 6:2). They may have missed the significance of what was happening. Bringing people together in Christ from all lifestyles and differing backgrounds was also part of serving the Word of God.

Through the guidance of the Spirit, they called on men from Greek backgrounds to handle this messy food-distribution ministry and to help bridge the cultural divide that had emerged. Two of these men were Stephen and Philip, who became more renowned for their preaching than their kitchen work and care for the poor.

Being Great according to Jesus's Standards

When Jesus taught his disciples about this radical definition of family and what it meant to be the church, he used children as props. After telling his disciples that if they want to be first they must learn to be the very last, and the servant of all, he used a little child as an illustration. Taking the child in his arms, he said, "Whoever welcomes one of these little children in my name welcomes me; and whoever welcomes me does not welcome me but the one who sent me" (Mark 9:35–37, NIV). Children were powerless in their world and completely dependent on others.

Welcoming children seems easier for us than thinking about folding lonely adults, outsiders, and outcasts into the bosoms of our families. Some of the teaching of Jesus puts people on the defensive because of his rigorous demands, but most will let down their guard when they hear this Word. We have received children in Jesus's name. We may have taught children's Sunday school classes. We may have taken our turn at nursery duty and changed children's diapers. We may have poured Kool-Aid and messed with glue and glitter in Vacation Bible School or Cub Scouts or Brownies. Some of us have fundamentally reordered our lives—our sleep, our daily tasks, our finances—around the little ones born into our own families.

Jesus was talking about more than teaching, enjoying, and welcoming children with a children's sermon during worship. He was teaching his disciples what counted and who counted in life. It was in this context of trying to teach the disciples about what it means to be great leaders that he brought a little one into their midst. He told them that if they wanted to be great, if they wanted to welcome God into their lives, then they had to become servants, to seek out and care for the nobodies. Still, what he meant did not sink into their heads. Shortly after this, people brought little children to Jesus for his blessing, and the disciples tried to block their access to him (Mark 10:13–14). They imagined that he had more important business to carry out than to bother with children, who, in the grand scheme of things, did not seem to matter all that much. The apostles did not understand that greatness for Jesus was *reaching* out for the *shut* out.

It was newcomers like Stephen and Philip who applied this lesson in their ministries. Frank Stagg claims:

> It is ironical that those who were too busy with "spiritual" matters to "serve tables" failed to provide the deeper insights into the gospel. . . . The twelve, who insisted that they must devote all their time to "prayer and the ministry of the word," were slow to see that with God there is "no respecter of persons." Stephen, Philip, and five others were mundane enough to be assigned this table-serving job, but somehow they—at least Stephen and Philip—developed the keenest insights into the gospel. (Stagg 1955, 89)

At the end of his ministry, the Sanhedrin hauled Stephen before them to answer charges. There he delivered the longest sermon in the Book of Acts. Like the message of Jesus before him, the message he brought was too radical for the establishment. As they began to stone him to death, Stephen saw the risen Christ standing in heaven, waiting to welcome him into the presence of God.

During the persecution that broke out after Stephen's death and the scattering of the church, Philip miraculously healed the sick and preached in Samaria to the much-hated Samaritans (see Luke 9:51–56). Together, Stephen and Philip blazed new mission trails, realizing that this Christian movement was intended to draw everybody into the family, no matter how powerless, poor, rich, or different they might be.

Alone on a Downhill Road

After Stephen's death, Philip, yet another designated to be a "table waiter" by the disciples, becomes the focus of attention in the narrative of Acts. Something about caring for the gathered extended family of faith at table gave him a vision for ministry. It is not either/or—care for the community of faith or respond to the needs beyond us; following Jesus always means doing both. Philip had the vision, and the nerve to match it, to preach in Samaria, where they received his healing ministry with great joy (Acts 8:8). After he had baptized the Samaritans, Peter and John followed Stephen into Samaria, praying for the new converts to receive the Holy Spirit (Acts 8:15–17, 25). Meanwhile, an angel called Philip even further afield to a new place, the downhill desert road that runs from Jerusalem to Gaza (Acts 8:26).

Traveling down the road from Jerusalem through the desert toward Gaza was an Ethiopian eunuch, an important official responsible for the treasury of the queen of the Ethiopians. For Luke's audience, a man from Ethiopia would be like saying in our context that he was from Timbuktu. He hailed from some distant, exotic land. He is identified first, however, as "a eunuch." He is nameless and identified only by his place of origin and his disability as a sexless person. In our more politically correct culture, we try never to label people by their disabilities. We would not call someone "the cripple," "the schizophrenic," or, as we have heard someone do in a nursing home, "the Alzheimer's in room 14." The ancient world was not polite. This man was known to all by his mutilation.

Eunuchs are not exactly topics of daily conversation these days. This man's condition reflects the brutality of a bygone day. Eunuchs tended to be slaves who were castrated to punish them for some offense, to subjugate them, or to make them safe so that they could attend faithfully to such duties as being in charge of the king's women (see Esther 2:3, 14–15). Royalty could safely promote them to higher levels of responsibility because they posed no threat of having children who might later attempt to usurp the throne. But this was small consolation for being emasculated. Insult was added to injury, because eunuchs were despised and derided in the ancient world as effeminate, forever betrayed by their beardless faces and high-pitched voices.

Lucian of Samosota, an ancient satirist, voiced the common opinion that eunuchs were freaks who could never be whole. He described them as neither man nor woman and declared it "an ill-omened, ill-met sight if on first leaving home in the morning one should set eyes on any such person [a eunuch]" (*The Eunuch* 6–11; cited by Spencer 1992, 157). The first-century Jewish historian Josephus ungraciously described them as "monstrosities" (Josephus, *Antiquities* 4 §§290–91), and Philo of Alexandria lumped them in with his discussion of the categories of "worthless persons" (*Special Laws* 1,324–325; see Spencer 1992, 157). They could never escape their shame or have a wife and children. This particular eunuch had risen in the ranks as the treasurer for his nation's queen. Nevertheless, his wealth and connection to power did not eradicate the shame and loneliness imposed on him by societal attitudes toward him. He is identified as a eunuch, as Mr. Cut-off, and some would question whether he deserved even being called a mister.

This man from black (see Jer. 13:23) Africa, modern-day Sudan (not Abyssinia), had traversed a great distance to worship the God of the Jews in Jerusalem, and now he was on his way home, reading out loud the Book of Isaiah and puzzling over what it meant. Why had he trekked all the way to Jerusalem? His mutilation denied him entrance into the temple. Deuteronomy 23:1 lays down the law: "No one whose testicles are crushed or whose penis is cut off shall be admitted to the assembly of the LORD." Did he make this journey, only to discover at the last minute that he was forever banned from entering the temple? At best, he could peek through the knotholes to get an idea of what was going on.

Today, it would be like someone barred from entering a church but showing up anyway and asking the worshipers as they returned to their cars in the parking lot, "Can I see the bulletin? How was the music? What was the sermon about?" F. Scott Spencer summarizes the plight of his status as a religious persona non grata: "without access to Israel's pivotal institution, the eunuch appeared to be excluded from the covenant community, hopelessly alienated from God's household—a status only punctuated by the eunuch's total incapacity to generate a family of his own" (Spencer 1992, 160).

Now he was headed back down the road to his far-away home, reading aloud to himself, as people did in that day. Barred from entering Israel's temple, he turned to Israel's scripture for illumination and hope. He read from a scroll of Isaiah, and he must have been wealthy enough to secure his own personal copy. It would have been quite an investment, but he must have thought that it was worth it. Was he wondering if the prophet Isaiah offered any hope for the likes of him? He was bouncing along in a chariot on a rough ancient road, reading a chapter that begins:

He had no beauty or majesty to attract us to him, nothing in his appearance that we should desire him. He was despised and rejected by men, a man of sorrows, and familiar with suffering. Like one from whom men hide their faces he was despised, and we esteemed him not. Surely he took up our infirmities and carried our sorrows, yet we considered him stricken by God, smitten by him, and afflicted. (Isaiah 53:2a–4)

He understood what it meant to be despised, rejected, and familiar with pain. Eagerly, he read on about this despised man by whose "wounds we are healed." "Who could this be?" he wondered. Is the prophet speaking about himself or someone else? He is both drawn to this scripture and puzzled by it. He needs someone to interpret it for him.

God sent Philip looking for him—him!—on this lonely stretch of wilderness road. The Holy Spirit moved Philip to sidle up to the eunuch's chariot. Led by the Spirit and knowing that God is no respecter of persons, Philip did not regard it "an ill-omened, ill-met sight" to meet up with a eunuch. As he approached the chariot, he heard the man reading aloud the familiar passage from Isaiah. He had reached a point in the prophet's word (Isa. 53:7–8) that Luke underscores by quoting it in his text:

Like a sheep he was led to the slaughter, and like a lamb silent before its shearer, so he does not open his mouth. In his humiliation justice was denied him. Who can describe his generation? For his life is taken away from the earth. (Acts 8:32–33)

It is easy to understand how a eunuch would be fascinated by and could resonate with this passage describing "a pathetic, sheep-like figure, slaughtered and shorn (cut), dead and dumb (weak of voice)—the victim of humiliation" (Spencer 1992, 158).

A lamb whose wool is *cut off,* who is humiliated and denied justice—that described him to a tee! But what did this phrase mean, "Who can describe his generation?" Luke uses the word here to describe the descendants, the generation of a family. The prophet's point, however, is "ambiguous." Spencer asks, "Is he lamenting the tragedy that the servant dies without progeny, with his family line 'cut off'? Or, striking a completely different tone, is Isaiah marveling at the surprising throng of descendants generated from the servant's humiliation and ultimate vindication? In other words, is the servant's generation 'indescribable' because it is *not worth mentioning* or because it is *too vast to calculate?*" (Spencer 1992, 160). The question of generating a family of descendants seared the eunuch's heart. No hope for him. Or was there?

Philip discerned the faint hope against hope in the question marks that punctuated his reading of the prophecy. Despite the eunuch's ornate chariot and the trappings of royalty that came with his high position in the queen's service, he still felt very much alone in life. Something in the quaver of the man's voice and the prompting of the Holy Spirit compelled Philip to run up and interrupt: "Do you understand what you are reading?" (Acts 8:31). The answer was obvious: "I haven't a clue."

To his surprise, the eunuch's wishful thinking that this passage might hold a key that would remove his shame and desolation was true. He was about to learn from Philip that he no longer was cut off from the family of God and no longer was left outside to peek in through the knotholes to see what was going on. When he invited Philip to jump up into the chariot and sit beside him to interpret the message of Isaiah, he learned that there was good news for someone like him. It was in this wilderness on the downhill road, leading *away* from the temple and the holy city with all of its recent bitter disappointment and exclusion, that he heard an incredible uplifting word.

Philip identified the suffering figure that Isaiah was describing as Jesus of Nazareth, recently scourged to a bloody pulp and hung on a cross to die the most humiliating of deaths, one reserved only for slaves and the dregs of society. But this horrifying death was not the end of the story. The good news was that God had raised him from the dead and exalted him on high. Being raised up by God did not mean simply that he was transported from this vale of tears to "a better place," but that he was glorified by God. It was a "radical social reversal": the "severest humiliation gives way ultimately to exaltation; shame is replaced by honor" (Spencer 1992, 158). God sent Philip to this man, this eunuch, to explain the good news about Jesus, the one without descendants, like the eunuch himself, but who has countless family members.

Admittedly, it is an odd family. One sees gathered into this household the poor, crippled, lame, and blind drawn from the boulevards and alleyways of the city and from the country roads and hedges of the hinterlands (Luke 14:15–24). It includes a condemned convict crucified with Jesus on a Roman cross (Luke 23:39–43) and a Roman centurion (Acts 10:17–48). It includes notorious sinners (Luke 7:36–50; 19:1–10) and those striving to be righteous (Luke 1:5–7; 23:50–52), as well as a bunch of hopeless social pariahs, now healed and restored (Luke 5:12–32; 8:26–39). Will it also include a eunuch?

The Ethiopian's first two questions—"How can I understand unless someone guides me?" "Who is the prophet talking about?"—have been answered. Now he asked a third question: "Look, here is water! What is to prevent me from being baptized?" (Acts 8:36). He wants to know if he can be included in this family too. The answer comes when Philip commands the chariot to stop, descends with the man, gets into the water with him, and baptizes him (Acts 8:38). The Ethiopian found a new home in the baptismal waters with Philip. Nothing stood in the way of this man being included in this new household that takes in all comers. In the baptismal waters he received a promise far better than the blessing of biological children.

Philip was suddenly gone, and the Ethiopian was left to go on his way, but he went now "rejoicing" (Acts 8:39). We might imagine that the man read on in Isaiah. There, just three chapters beyond where he was reading when Philip joined him, this man finds his own name:

> Do not let the foreigner joined to the LORD say, "The LORD will surely separate me from his people"; and do not let the *eunuch* say, "I am just a dry tree." For thus says the LORD: "To the *eunuchs* who keep my sabbaths, who choose the things that please me and hold fast my covenant, I will give, in my house and within my walls, a monument and a name better than sons and daughters; I will give them an everlasting name *that shall not be cut off.*" (Isa. 56:3–5, italics added)

That was who he was, a foreigner and a eunuch. But he learned that in Jesus, he was no longer excluded, no longer an outsider, no longer a "dry," fruitless tree standing alone. Excluded from the Jerusalem temple, he is included in this new household of God centered on Christ's sacrifice, which provides a home for the homeless and a family for those without family.

One can only presume that he spread the good news of Christ when he arrived back home. His descendants are those whom he brought to the faith by his testimony. The unmarried Paul had many children by this means, and he calls Onesimus "my child whom I begot in prison" (authors' translation) by virtue of converting him to faith in Christ (Philemon 10; see also 1 Tim. 1:2; Titus 1:4; 1 Cor. 4:14–15; Gal. 4:19; 1 Thess. 2:11).

Being widowed, divorced, unmarried, or unable to conceive children does not exclude one from having family. Jesus promised that if one follows him, one could be part of the family. When we experience being cut off, the mutilation caused by divorce, separation, infidelity, rejection, the death of a spouse, we still belong to Jesus. In following Jesus, we find loving brothers and sisters and mothers and children beyond imagining.

Tragically, the church today has been captured by a culture that limits family to biological and marital relationships. In 2005, Christmas day fell on a Sunday. Many churches decided to shut their doors on Sunday morning so that their ministry staff might spend time with their families. We heard the young wife of a minister at a large church that had decided to hold services on Christmas morning lament that it was not fair for the ministers and staff to have to come to church and miss this precious time with family. She said, "No one will be there. The only people who will come are the singles and the old people without families." A single adult who was not involved in a church herself overheard this and was shocked. "I thought the church was to be the place where those without families could go and find a home," she said later. "Isn't the church supposed to be the home for the homeless, the family for the family-less?" People ask those who recently have moved to town—at least they do so in Waco, Texas—"Have you found a church home yet?"

We may call the church a "home," but the church, like our larger culture, tends to name families by their parts. We need to have a husband and wife in a first marriage to be a whole and perfect family. If anything has been cut off, then we are labeled, like the eunuch, by what is no longer there or by what we think should be there. We are a single-parent family, a divorced family, a stepfamily, a widow, a single adult. Long-term marriages and biological parenting are wonderful blessings; we certainly can testify to that from our thirty-six years together and the joy our children bring us. Paul uses marriage as a beautiful metaphor to describe Jesus's love for the church (Eph. 5:21–33). Marriage and children are only one way to be blessed with family. In fact, families created anew from brokenness are the *best* pictures of God's good news. This man, first known as a eunuch, is a witness to the way God can make wholeness out of brokenness—can give someone who will never have children the promise of being re-membered as a part of the family.

This good news is not only for eunuchs; it is for all who have experienced brokenness in life. It is for those who are recreating family after death or divorce or unwanted child-lessness. In the community of faith, families should never be defined as "broken" because a marriage has ended, for example. Calling them "broken" seems to imply that they belong in the scratched and dented half-price bin or are des-tined to be thrown away and to end up in some landfill with other shattered families. As a young divorced mother said, "The church calls me and my son a broken family. But I have moved on, and in Christ I don't feel broken; I feel whole." Indeed, that is Jesus's promise that we can be made new, whole, even "perfect" all over again.

Are Perfect Families Normal?

In today's culture, we think of "the perfect family" as a first marriage and a baby or two who turn out to be good people and successful adults. Perfect families smile a lot. They show up at church on Sunday morning looking trouble-free, with no sign of the squabbling and bickering that may have peppered the early-morning struggle to get out the door on time. They show no signs of the worries about finances that created suppertime quarrels or the anxieties over how best to care for a parent with Alzheimer's disease. When Jesus told us to "be perfect" (Matt. 5:43–48), he was not talking about getting married and having beautiful babies and expecting life to be full of smiles and struggle-free, or at least to pretend that it is. He was talking about loving enemies, namely, acting toward them in such a way that we show preference to them. "The perfection that is required is not moral flawlessness but the perfection of love that reaches out to one and all, neighbor and enemy, indiscriminately" (Garland 2001, 77).

One of the richest experiences of my (Diana's) life has been interviewing families to learn about how faith shapes the family life of Christians. I have told their stories in another book (2003), but two of their stories bear repeating here.

Dan was sixteen years old when I first met him. Dan lived with his mother, Ms. Coper, and his four-year-old brother, Joe, in a ranch house in an integrated suburb of a midwestern American city. They are African American and drive more than twenty minutes each direction to stay actively involved in their black, inner-city congregation. Their congregation is developing its community and battling social problems that plague their city. Ms. Coper knew that I was writing a book about families, and that their congregation had welcomed me into their fellowship. I knocked on the front door late on a Sunday afternoon; I had an appointment to talk with Ms. Coper about their family as a part of my research. I was met at the door by Dan, an imposing figure, standing 6 feet 5 inches tall, and strong, a football player. He was surprised and a little puzzled to see me; his mother had not told him that I was coming. Even so, he graciously invited me in, offered me a cola, and stayed to talk with me until his mother came home. She had gone out to lunch with her sisters and had not yet returned.

Joe, I learned, is not Dan's biological brother but rather Ms. Coper's cousin's baby. Joe's mother is mentally ill, so Ms. Coper has custody of Joe. Ms. Coper is a single mother with a clerical job. For a few months after Dan was born, sixteen years ago, Ms. Coper was on welfare, but she now has a very good job and she owns their home. Dan told me a lot about his family, about his own near-scrapes with trouble, about how his mother "dragged" him to the pastor for a few "little talks" about his behavior, and then started him with karate lessons to teach him self-discipline and how to channel his strength and energy in positive ways. Every morning, she prays over him before he leaves for school.

The garage door opening announced Ms. Coper's arrival, and Dan was relieved to be able to hand off the conversation to his mother when she rushed in, apologizing for being late. We talked into the evening, as she filled out more of their story. They really had endured some hard times. Money was tight when Dan was a baby, and she was even homeless with him for awhile. She still struggled sometimes; it is not easy for a mother to raise sons by herself. Yet she is currently offering informal foster care to a little girl in the neighborhood who will otherwise be placed in a foster home in another area of the city and have to change schools.

Before his mother arrived, I had asked Dan to tell me about what role, if any, faith plays in their family life. He said, "No matter what happens, my mom always pays her tithe, even if it is all the money she has, and we go to church mostly every Sunday. She believes in God a whole lot. That's why she's so comfortable with being single, because I don't think anybody else could do it the way she does it. I think my brother and I *are* her social life."

He went on to tell me that not only does his mother provide a home for himself and Joe and now a foster child, but she folds into her life the teenagers in the church:

> My mom and her friend work with the church youth group. They would have meetings and talk about STDs [sexually transmitted diseases], sex, and all kinds of stuff that nags at us—gangs, violence and everything. It helped some of them out a lot. It really didn't affect me, because I always thought that, besides my father being gone, I had the perfect home.

The word *perfect* hit me. But the world tells him that his family cannot be perfect if there is no father there, Dan feels something in their life together that is *perfect*. He is right. His mother lives an impossible love. Managing on a financial shoestring, she is raising not only her biological son but two more children as well. She is living impossible perfection, sustained by faith and challenging the church to be good news for all its children.

In the same city, but far from the suburbs where Ms. Coper lives, James and Marianne brought three children to their marriage from their previous marriages. They are African American, living in a predominantly African American inner-city neighborhood. James's nineteen-year-old son, Corey, has severe developmental and physical challenges and uses a wheelchair; he works part-time at a sheltered workshop. Marianne has two daughters, Sasha (16) and Sandi (11), and the year before I visited them, the "ours" baby, Ariah, was born.

The family lives just beyond poverty, literally. Just around the corner from them is one of the most physically decaying, gang-infested public housing projects in their city. James works there as a maintenance man. He sees it as his mission field. Each time he knocks on a door to go in and fix the plumbing or the wiring, he prays that he will treat the resident as if that resident were Jesus. "Feed my sheep." Marianne prays for his mission to the residents of the housing project, for his courage and witness and safety. She works as a secretary downtown.

They are proud to own their two-story house, which they consider an anchor for their community along with the homes of several other church members nearby. Although their house is just around the block from poverty, it is located on a quiet street. Like the few other church-member-owned houses on the street, the cheerful new coat of paint and the flowers planted by the front fence say that James and Marianne's house is a home, and that they are there to stay and encourage others to be community for one another.

Life has not always been so full of promise, however. Shortly after their marriage five years before, James lost the job he had at the time, and the only other work he could find was as a bartender. In discouragement, he slipped into alcohol and drug abuse, sometimes not coming home at night. But that was then. When I visited them, he had been years on the road to recovery from addiction after a profound religious conversion. He spoke of his love for their congregation and their pastor, and he was in training to become a deacon. They were spending much of the time they were not working involved in church activities with their children, and helping with the church's many programs designed to stabilize the community and tackle its complex problems of poverty and hopelessness.

How did they survive? One of my questions to families I interviewed was, "Tell me a Bible story that you especially identify with." Marianne responded that she thinks she is a bit like Moses's wife:

> She just stuck with him being gone up to the mountain, waiting for him to come back down. That's how I look at

myself. I'm there for my husband through thick and thin. I came close to giving up, because I kept thinking when we were going through it, "I'm just going to tell him to get out, to leave." Then I thought, "No, because if I tell him that, he'll really do it. If I tell him to leave, he won't come home." Through all of what was happening, I kept praying and praying and praying. It just made me stronger. One of my nieces told me one day, "You just think you are the perfect family, don't you?"

"No, we're not," she chuckled deeply and then laughed out loud at the thought of being a perfect family. Sandi, the eleven-year old, joined in the conversation: "I know who I'm like. I'm like David, because he fought Goliath with only five stones. And Goliath had a sword and shield, and David killed him with just one stone. I think I'm as strong as David, and I can do anything with Christ." Sandi echoed the family theme, "we do all things through Christ who strengthens us," based on Philippians 4:13. Mom had lived through her husband's days of drugging and not supporting his family and not even coming home. Dad found his way through the alcohol and drugs, sustained by his wife's prayers. And the children learned that they, too, can slay the giants that threaten them. Given all they have been through, Marianne laughed at the thought of being called perfect. It is not a likely word to describe a family shaped by the forces that have shaped them. Her laugh was not just of disbelief—it was also a deep belly laugh of recognition. Her niece had hit on an element of deeper truth, that there is a process of perfection at work here.

Perfection is not about being problem-free. Perfection is about allowing and celebrating God's work through us, and James and Marianne have given God plenty of opportunity to work in their lives. The apostle Paul begged the Lord to take away whatever he experienced as some fault or problem sent to him to keep him from being conceited, some "thorn . . . in the flesh, a messenger of Satan," that tormented him (2 Cor. 12:7). Some weakness burdened him, and we can only guess what it was. We do know the answer he received from the Lord. When he implored the Lord repeatedly to remove this weakness, the answer he received was, "My grace is sufficient for you, for power is made perfect in weakness" (2 Cor. 12:9a). Paul goes on to say, "So, I will boast all the more gladly of my weaknesses, so that the power of Christ may dwell in me. Therefore I am content with weaknesses, insults, hardships, persecutions, and calamities for the sake of Christ; for whenever I am weak, then I am strong" (2 Cor. 12:9b–10). Through some divine alchemy, God turns our weakness and struggles into something "perfect." God takes broken families of all kinds of shapes and sizes and works processes of perfection through them. Whoever we are, in whatever kind of family, we too can boast with Paul, can laugh with Marianne, can rise up out of baptismal water and go on our way rejoicing in the promise of God's family with a man who used to be called "a eunuch." We are no longer defined by brokenness but by redemption. It is the great challenge of the church today to be the Good News family Jesus promised to those journeying alone on lonely downhill roads and wondering, "Who is this lamb?"

References Cited

Alsdurf, James M., and Phyllis Alsdurf. 1988. A pastoral response. In *Abuse and religion: When praying isn't enough,* edited by Anne L. Horton and Judith A. Williamson, 165–71. Lexington, MA: Lexington Books.

Alter, Robert. 1981. *The art of biblical narrative.* New York: Basic Books.

Arnold, Bill T. 2003. *1 & 2 Samuel.* NIV Application Commentary. Grand Rapids: Zondervan.

Bird, Phyllis A. 1989. The harlot as heroine: Narrative art and social presupposition in three Old Testament texts. *Semeia* 46:119–39.

Bos, Johanna W. H. 1992. An eyeopener at the gate: George Coats and Genesis 38. *Lexington Theological Quarterly* 27:119–23.

Brock, Rita Nakashima, Rebecca Ann Parker, David Blumenthal, Traci C. West, Jung Ha Kim, and Marie M. Fortune. 2002. A witness for/from life: Writing feminist theology as an act of resisting violence—Responses to *Proverbs of ashes: Violence, redemptive suffering, and the search for what saves us. Journal of Religion & Abuse* 4 (2):69–96.

Browne, Angela. 1988. Family homicide. In *Handbook of family violence*, edited by Vincent B. Van Hasselt, Randall L. Morrison, Alan S. Bellack, and Michel Hersen, 271–89. New York: Plenum Press.

Carter, Forrest. 1976. *The education of Little Tree.* Albuquerque: University of New Mexico Press.

Chambers, Oswald. 1963. *My utmost for his highest.* New York: Dodd, Mead.

David and Bathsheba, released by 20th Century Fox, 1951, directed by Henry King, produced by Darryl F. Zanuck. DVD released through 20th Century Fox, 2006.

Davis, Ila Marie, with Evelyn Stenbock-Ditty. *A gleam of light: The trials and triumphs of a century of missionary work in Morocco.* Kansas City, MO: Gospel Missionary Union, 1998.

The Divine Secrets of the Ya Ya Sisterhood, released by All Girl Productions, Gaylord Films, 2002, directed by Callie Khouri, produced by Bonnie Bruckheimer. DVD released through Warner Home Video, 2003.

Dunn, Stephen. 1989. *Between angels.* New York: Norton.

Edghill, India. 2002. *Queenmaker: A novel of King David's queen.* New York: St. Martin's.

Falk, Marcia. 1994. Reflections on Hannah's prayer. *Tikkun* 9:61–64.

Flynn, Clifton P. 1990. Relationship violence by women: Issues and implications. *Family Relations* 39 (2):194–98.

Flynn, Kathryn A. 2003. *The sexual abuse of women by members of the clergy.* Jefferson, NC: McFarland.

Fortune, Marie M. 1995. Forgiveness: The last step. In *Violence against women and children.* Edited by Carol J. Adams and Marie M. Fortune, 201–6. New York: Continuum.

Fuchs, Esther. 1989. Marginalization, ambiguity, silencing: The story of Jephthah's daughter. *Journal of Feminist Studies in Religion* 5:35–45.

Garland, David E. 1996. *Mark*. NIV Application Commentary. Grand Rapids: Zondervan.

———. 2001. *Reading Matthew: A literary and theological commentary*. Macon, GA: Smyth and Helwys.

Garland, Diana R. 2003. *Sacred stories of ordinary families: Living the faith in daily life*. San Francisco: Jossey-Bass.

de Groot van Houten, Christiana. 1997. The rape of the concubine. *Perspectives* 12:12–15.

Gunn, David M. 1978. The story of King David: Genre and interpretation. *Journal for the Study of the Old Testament*, supplement 6. Sheffield: Department of Biblical Studies, University of Sheffield.

———. 1996. Bathsheba goes bathing in Hollywood: Words, images, and social locations. *Semeia* 74:97–98.

Halpern, Baruch. 2001. *David's secret dreams: Messiah, murderer, traitor, king*. Grand Rapids: Eerdmans.

Horst, Elisabeth A. 1998. *Recovering the lost self: Shame-healing for victims of clergy sexual abuse*. Collegeville, MN: Order of St. Benedict.

Kaplan, E. Ann. 1983. *Women in film: Both sides of the camera*. London: Routledge.

Lamott, Anne. 1994. *Bird by bird: Some instructions on writing and life*. New York: Anchor.

———. 1999. *Traveling mercies: Some thoughts on faith*. New York: Pantheon.

McCarter, P. Kyle Jr. 1984. *II Samuel*. Anchor Bible, vol. 9. Garden City, NY: Doubleday.

Miller, Dusty. 2003. The end of innocence: Reconsidering our concepts of victimhood. *Psychotherapy Networker* 27 (4): 24–33.

Nouwen, Henri J. M. 2001. The path of waiting. In *Finding my way home: Pathways to life and the Spirit*, 92–119. New York: Crossroad.

Pagelow, Mildred Daley. 1988. Marital rape. In *Handbook of family violence*. Edited by Vincent B. Van Hasselt, Randall L. Morrison, Alan S. Bellack, and Michel Hersen, 207–32. New York: Plenum Press.

Pipher, Mary. 2003. Advice to a young therapist: Learning to trust the wisdom of the family. *Psychotherapy Networker* 27 (5):58–63.

Prince of Tides, released by Columbia Pictures, 1991, directed by Barbara Streisand, produced by Cis Corman. The video is available through Columbia Tristar Home Video, 1992.

Prosser, Bo. 2006. The changing shape of family. *Christian Reflection* 19:62–65.

Rohr, Richard. 1995. Changing the world is an inside job. *Salt of the Earth* 15 (3):17–19.

Rose, Susan D. 2002. Telling lives: Trauma-recovery and Christian-conversion narratives. *Journal of Religion & Abuse* 4 (2):33–68.

Rothschild, Babette. 2004. Applying the brakes. *Psychotherapy Networker* 28 (1):42–45, 66–67.

Russell, Diana E. H. 1984. *Sexual exploitation: Rape, child sexual abuse and workplace harassment*. Beverly Hills, CA: Sage.

Rutter, Peter. 1989. *Sex in the forbidden zone: When men in power— therapists, doctors, clergy, teachers, and others—betray women's trust*. New York: Fawcett Columbine.

Sakenfeld, Katharine Doob. 2003. *Just wives: Stories of power and survival in the Old Testament and today*. Louisville: Westminster/John Knox Press.

Schepps, David. 1976. *Remarkable women of the scriptures*. Philadelphia: Dorrance.

Shanks, Hershel. 2006. Wrestling with Scripture. *Biblical Archaeological Review* 30 (2): 46–52, 76.

Smith, Carol. 1992. The story of Tamar: A power-filled challenge to the structures of power. In *Women in the Biblical*

Tradition, edited by George J. Brooke, 16–28. Studies in Women and Religion, vol. 31. Lewiston/Queenston/Lampeter: Mellen.

Spencer, F. Scott. 1992. The Ethiopian eunuch and his Bible: A social-science analysis. *Biblical Theological Bulletin* 22:155–65.

Stagg, Frank. 1955. *The book of Acts: The early struggle for an unhindered gospel.* Nashville: Broadman.

Sundberg, Walter. 1993. Jephthah's daughter: An invitation to non-lectionary preaching. *Word & World* 13 (1): 85–90.

Taylor, Barbara Brown. 1998. *God in pain: Teaching sermons on suffering.* Nashville: Abingdon.

Trible, Phyllis. 1981. A meditation in mourning: The sacrifice of the daughter of Jephthah. *Union Seminary Quarterly Review* 36:59–73.

———. 1984. *Texts of terror: Literary-feminist readings of biblical narratives.* Philadelphia: Fortress.

Vanauken, Sheldon. 1977. *A severe mercy.* San Francisco: Harper and Row.

Willimon, William H. 1998. *Reading with deeper eyes: The love of literature and the life of faith.* Nashville: Upper Room Books.

Yllo, Kesrti, and Donna LeClerc. 1988. Marital rape. In *Abuse and religion: When praying isn't enough.* Edited by Anne L. Horton and Judith A. Williamson, 48–57. Lexington, MA: Lexington Books.